Prologue

My generation, known as "the most prepared in our history", was forced to emigrate in search of better opportunities. Many endorsed the expression "we don't leave, they kick us out" to show their frustation with the goverment and their policies.

But it wasn't the first time, neither won't be the last. I know how hard is to leave behind your country, your people, but I firmly believe that we had an incredible opportunity.

I remember that in the 60s, nearly a million Spaniards were forced to emigrate to Germany. Those are the ones who suffered, those who had really a hard time, those who deserved to be praised. Compared to them, we are a privileged generation.

We must never forget that.

1 | One way ticket

"Today is the day" I repeated myself on my way to the airport. It seemed to me that moment would never arrive. Gone are the days of goodbyes, the doubts, the long hours thinking what might go wrong, "there is no way back, today is the day".

Like many other young Spaniards, I decided to emigrate in 2012 in search of a better future. I had spent all summer doing interviews and finally got a job in Austria, in a company that fulfill what I was looking for.

I remember my last few weeks in Spain as a continuous battle against a flood of thoughts that constantly reminded me what could go wrong, how difficult all it would be, who knows, maybe even impossible. I was trying to convince myself that everything would be alright, but it was too much. I just wanted the day to come and start dealing with everything.

I had arrived at the airport more than in time, when I got to the boarding gate, it still left 2 hours to be opened. "You never know what can happen" I thought when I was planning the trip.

I decided then to make the best of that time. I took my German grammar out of my backpack and started to study.

While I was immersed in that jungle of vocabulary, rules and exceptions, I realized that sitting next to me, an old man was staring at me. I didn't pay much attention to him and checked again my boarding pass, passport, etc. It looked like I had everything under control.

I returned to my grammar but the was still looking at me, now smiling slightly. He turned towards me and said:

"Where in Austria, Jose?"

"Excuse me?"

"To work, where in Austria are you going work?".

I was confused, and quite sure I didn't know him, but he apparently knew me. While I was still wondering who the man could be, I replied: "Vorarlberg. Tomorrow I start working in Klaus, Vorarlberg".

"Ahhhh Vorarlberg, great area, I love it, they have the best Käsespätzle in the world!!"

"Sorry, the best what?".

"Oh nothing, don't worry, you'll find out soon" said while laughing and then he went back to his reading.

Still confused, I returned to my grammar, but I couldn't stop thinking who this man was and how he could possibly know my name. I don't take it anymore and asked him: "Excuse me, do we know each other?".

"Oh sorry, where are my manners?, my name is Corbalán, pleased to meet you".

That name didn't ring a bell. "How do you know my name? And why Austria?, why not Germany or Switzerland?, why to work and not on vacation?"

And that old man, endearing and cheerful, looked at me as if I was a child asking if the Earth orbits around the sun or the other way around.

"Son, your name is everywhere. It's in the papers you don't stop looking, in the passport you're constantly checking. So stressed and nervous, it must be because is the first time you go wherever you're going and why, whatever you're going to do there, is very important for you".

"Besides, lots of young Spaniards are moving abroad in last years, right?" he said.

I noticed how I began to feel more stupid. Meanwhile he continued with his deduction."You're reading a German grammar. Nobody goes on vacation with a German grammar as bedside reading. So chances are, you're going to work".

"And you're waiting for a flight to Zürich, right?. You've looked at the gate a thousand times so far. If you were flying to Germany you would chosen Munich as destination. You could fly to Switzerland, that's true, but in Switzerland nobody is hiring Spaniards unless they know the language, trust me, I live there. So finally, it's almost sure that you're going to Austria".

It took me a few seconds to put myself together, but that man, without knowing me, kept asking what I was expecting from Austria, from that trip, and finally I told him everything that was crossing my mind.

That old man, Corbalán, was a Spanish who had spent his youth in Spain and had emigrated to Germany in the 60s, like many others. Few years later he had moved to Switzerland, where he met his wife. Now retired, he lived between Spain and Switzerland.

"You know, there are so many things... the language, culture, I know is not going to be simple" I said.

"You're wrong, it is simple".

"That's easy for you to say, after so many years, of course it seems simple to you".

"No, I mean it's simple. Not easy, but simple".

I didn't fully understand what he meant, but he continued with his explanation: "For example, the language. It's simple to learn the language, the more time you spend on it, the faster you"ll learn it. But it's not easy, it's hard, if it were easy everybody would do it".

"And it has a cost, of course it does. But it'll be you, only you who will decide what's going to be, a punishment, an adventure, whatever you want. Don't forget it, only you will decide what's going to be. The best advice I can give you is,design a funny life, everything else is not worth".

We were interrupted by the public address announcing that the boarding was begun and I started feeling nervous again.

Meanwhile, Corbalán wrote something on a piece of paper. I gave it to me and said: "Here you go, this is my email, drop me a line from time to time, I would like to know how are you doing in Vorarlberg, ok?"

I took the paper and it said: life.is.good.in.austria@gmail.com. "It must be a joke"I thought. But again, that man read me again like an open book."It's real, seriously, text me, I will answer you" he replied.

We said goodbye and I went to the gate, hoping that everything was in order and there were no surprises. I was so nervous in the past days that I had imagined everything that could go wrong.

But as soon as I got on the airplane, I started calming down and feeling more relaxed. I began to be aware that the moment had finally arrived, I was leaving.

On the airplane one could listen German and Spanish equally among the passengers, I wondered that if in the future I would be like those people, belonging to two countries, two cultures at the same time.

Maybe someday. That idea motivated me a lot. I wanted to make every second count so I went back to my German grammar, with an unprecedented momentum.

The pilot announced the imminent takeoff and I left my book for a moment to look out the window and say good-bye to my country. It wasn't a drama, on the contrary, I was doing what I always wanted to do.

During the flight, I kept thinking about the words of Socratesİ couldn't get them out of my head. I tried to concentrate on the grammar but the accumulated stress in the recent days defeaed me and I fell asleep. Normally, I don't remember what I dream, but still today I remember clearly what I dreamed during that flight.

I was in a TV quiz show in which me, as a participant, I was competing against another guy who looked a lot like me but kind of angry and bitter. The audience applauded while waiting the entrance of the presenter. Beside m,e a stewardess whispered to me"Smile. Salute and smile". Meanwhile, my opponent waved to the crowd and faced those who rebuked him.

Finally, announced by the public address system and going through a cloud of smoke, the presenter came on the scene. Immaculate, white teeth, tanned skin. He calmed down the public and after pertinent greetings, he proceeded to explain the rules of the contest:

"Both participants must provide answers to the question of the day, and you, dear public, will decide who is our winner. Then, shall we start?. Here is today's question: What can happen to us in the coming months in Austria ?"

I didn't know what to answer to that, but my opponent seemed to have no doubts and said:

"They will fire us...".

"They won't understand us...".

"We will be ripped off...".

And the public, even though resigned, applauded him while his score was rising. It seemed that no one was aware of my presence until I decided to take action.

"We will learn to ski and we will love it" I said.

There was silence on the set. My opponent looked at the audience, then to my rising score and tried to fight back.

"We don't like heights, we won't even be able to get on the lift" he said.

"You can stay at home if you want, but I'm getting on" I replied decidedly.

And for the first time, the public began to applaud me.

"We will learn the language" I continued.

"It will take us years and it will be very boring" he said while turning to the audience seeking for their complicity.

I took my time to respond, I looked at presenter and sentenced: "We will learn just by doing tandems with girls".

The public applauded and cheered as never before. They had already decided their winner.

The presenter came to congratulate me and suddenly I woke up from my dream. I opened his eyes, the flight attendant was beside me, checking that everything was in order. We were about to land.

I got off the plane and on my way to pick up the suitcase, I was observing everything around me without losing any detail. After a short wait that felt eternal, I took the suitcase and went to the customs office.

I was so nervous and observing that even the officers found my behavior suspicious, they stopped me, inspected my luggage and let me go once they checked that everything was in order.

After that, I headed to the airport entrance looking for the taxi driver who was supossed to pick me up. I saw him in the distance with a sign saying "Mr. Collera". As I was approaching him, he realized and began waving me effusively while trying to pronounce my name, which sounded in Spanish like, "Mr. Colleague!, Mr. Colleague!".

My new friend didn't speak a word of English, so we couldn't have a proper conversation during the hour and a half that lasted the driving till the hotel.

We arrived at the hotel and he told me something in German that I couldn't understand, but judging by his expression, I figured he was wishing me good luck. I went into my room and prepared everything for the next day, my first day at my new job. I was so nervous that I could barely sleep.

2 | Orientation days

Since the first day I began to be aware of the particularities of Vorarlberg. I needed just half an hour to get to the office, but it was time enough to compare what I was seeing and what I knew from Spain.

I was living in Dornbirn, one of the largest cities in the region but with a population of 40,000 citizens. In that part of Austria there were not large cities but many small towns all not far away from each other. The office was located in an even smaller one, 1000 citizens. Soon I realized that a car was not necessary here, the public transport worked very well, there were many connections, services were usually punctual. The first few days I could not help thinking that while my friends were taking the subway in Madrid or Barcelona to go to work, I was on a train watching the snow-capped mountains.

The goal for those first days was mainly meet the people, the team. At that time, I wasn't aware of how lucky I was to be part of that team. To be honest, there was no way I could possibly know since I had assumed that all teams were similar to that but soon I learned that it wasn't like that.

The greatest advantage for me was that I was the only foreigner within a very sociable group. A group where everybody cared about each other. They helped me a lot at the beginning, so much that they made my first weeks and months very pleasant.

Most of them knew something about Spain, a bit of the language, some parts of the country, most of them had spent some holidays there in the past.

Every conversation was done in English, nobody had problems with that. Certainly, that made my first steps very easy. The topics were recurrent and in the end I was always talking about the same things and answering the same questions, what I was thinking about Austria so far, what was the opinion my family about that, how long I was intended to stay, etc.

So they were indeed very interesting weeks. And also intense, very intense. I remember going to bed exhausted most of the days, it required a lot of energy speaking English all day long, working, and also studying German.

Each small step was definitely a challenge and each piece of progress something to celebrate, no matter how small it was.

One of the first Austrian guys I met was Bernard. He constantly complained that I wasn't able to pronounce his name correctly, so I decided to call him Barnie. Barnie was in love with Spain, its people and its culture.

He could speak a bit of Spanish, less than he believed and he liked to tell stories about the time he had happened in Spain and the amount of girls he met there.

At first I was impressed about that, I even respected him for that. Given the introverted character of the Austrians compared to the Spaniards, I found it astonishing that he could adapted to our culture so fast and even succeeded with some girls. "This Barnie must be a crack, no doubt about it" I thought.

Eventually, I found out that his experience in Spain had been more discreet than he explained. In fact, it consisted of a vacation trip that had made with his family in Mallorca, two weeks to be exact.

And about women, one day that their parents were out for dinner and left him alone, he joined a group of English people in which there was a Scottish girl who spoke a bit of Spanish.

Confused by the rum and tequila, the Scottish girl took Barnie to the beach and they had there their special moment. Never before few minutes of glory gave birth to so many stories as those for Barnie.

But deep inside, I liked him, he was nice to me and quite cheerful, he contributed to make my first weeks more pleasant. With the arrival of Christmas, some markets emerged diary along the city, a great novelty for me, but I loved them. Cozy, cheerful and a sweet warm wine as a typical drink, the *gluhwein*.

That fit with the idea that I had about the Austrian people, always so kind, greeting to all people no matter if they know them or not. But since the beginning I was surprised by the ease they had to distinguish me as foreigner.

Everyone talked to me in English, receptionists, cashiers, even a guy who stopped me on the street asking me fire. I thought: "Maybe it's because here they all know each other".

But one day, while waiting for Barnie in a Christmas market, in the middle of a snow storm, I saw an old lady staring at me, probably confusing me with her grandson. The lady approached me and asked me in perfect Spanish:

"Excuse me, you are Spaniard, right?".

"Yeah... I am Spanish... how can you tell?" I replied a bit confused.

The lady pointed out politely my white sneakers and said: "Even if it's snowing you're wearing sneakers, definitely not from here, neither from some place where it snows regularly. Moreover, lots of Spaniards are moving recently to Vorarlberg, it isn't the first time I see something like this".

That was why people always spoke to me in English, it was clear that I was a foreigner. I decided then to pay more attention how the people dressed here, I wanted to go unnoticed, just like another Austrian guy.

The first step was easy, forget the sneakers and get a pair of good boots, no more slips and and more grip and while walking on snow. I went to a store and after seeing several models I decided to buy a pair of maroon boots with white and red laces, like the Austrian flag.

I was so confidence that I decided to test myself again. I went to the supermarket and I approached the cash deck, treading strongly so the cashier could appreciate my new boots. But it didn't work as I expected, as soon as it was my turn, the cashier greeted me coldly with a "Hello".

I didn't came down and kept thinking till I found my mistake, I was missing a cap. Everyone wears a cap when it's snowing. So I returned to the store and bought a cap. I tried again with a different cashier, but it didn't work, again as cold as her partner, the cashier said to me "Hello".

And standing there, watching the other customers, I was aware of my mistake. The Austrian customers greeted her with the typical "*Servus*" from here. I waited a few days and went again to the supermarket with my Austrian boots, the Austrian cap and the Austrian greeting well learned and practiced.

"Servus!" I said.

"Hello" she replied.

At that time, the frustration took control of me and I asked the cashier: "Hello? why Hello?, please explain it to me because I don't get, I'm wearing boots, hat, I've said Servus...".

"Yes, but you're not from here".

"Ok, but tell me, how can you possibly know?".

And the cashier looked at me, up and down, looking for something characteristic of a foreigner but found nothing. She didn't seem to care too much because with the same coldness of the first day, she stated: "I don't know, I think it's something in your face...".

Resigned, I just wanted to escape from there: "Ok, leave it, I don't like this game anymore. Thanks".

Some days later I told the story to Barnie. What a big mistake. My failure was the confirmation of his theory about how few chances of success an Spanish guy could have in Austria. According to him, it was very difficult, if not impossible, for a Spaniard to adapt to Vorarlberg, even more difficult to seduce an Austrian woman.

He used to say that we just simply hadn't the necessary skills, skills that obviously he had. He was convinced that in Spain everything was easier. Vorarlberg was another level, more difficult, more sophisticated. Hence, used to such difficult environment, he explained why he had triumphed so easily during his time in Spain.

The rest of the week, every conversation with him went around his theory. Every morning we caught the train to go to work. Just 15 minutes that gave us time to catch up and knowing each other better.

But one day, during the monologue of Barnie about how skillful one must be in order to integrate in Austria, the karma decided to give me a chance for revenge.

As the train approached its first stop, something caught the attention of Barnie, who suddenly fell silent while staring out the window:

"What's wrong Barnie?, You're scaring me" I said.

"Holy sheet, I can't believe what I'm seeing".

"What is it?, tell me, what do you see?".

"On the platform, the perfect woman is there, on the platform".

I looked out the window and I recognized the girl, she lived in the same building as me. I didn't know her name but I have greeted her already a couple of times. The train stopped and the girl came into our car. I turned to her so she could see me. She recognized me and approached us.

Barnie, nervous, started to whisper: "she's coming, oh my God, she's coming..." and I told him "Barnie, I know her, she's Austrian, I met her last weekend in a bar and we were talking all night long". He couldn't believe that.

As the girl walked towards us, Barnie paled more and more. She asked if the seat was free and sat with us.

At first, Barnie was looking at her really nervous, waiting for me to introduce him. But when he realized that I wasn't talking to her, he knew I was fooling him and his nerves turned into hate towards me.

Barnie was part of the team in which I was working, a group of nice and friendly people, who didn't fit the idea that I have about the local people, very serious and direct.

During those first weeks, I used to ask my colleagues all kind of questions, as expected since everything was new to me. My English wasn't too good at that time, which led from time to time to some misunderstandings.

Most of my questions were replied by one of my colleagues, an Austrian guy, one of those people with whom it's very easy to talk. I used to wonder if I was abusing of his kindness, because there were days that he spent so much time just helping me.

One day I asked him through the chat tool: "Do you know where can I find the use documentation?".

"It's in the project folder" he answered.

"FYI: The technical documentation is also there" he added.

And at that time I didn't know the meaning of "FYI", and I was worried about asking too much and wasting his time, so I didn't ask.

My colleague kept writing to me "FYI: Tomorrow I don't come to the office".

I kept thinking about the meaning of those acronyms until I came to the conclusion that it meant "Fuck You Idiot". Now everything made sense, he was upset and annoyed with me.

Later I wrote him again: "Hey sorry, can I make you a question?".

"Tell me. FYI: I have a meeting in five minutes".

Now it was clear, he was really angry with me, I must do something to fix the situation. I went to his office and to my surprise he greeted me cheerfully "Ohhh Jose, for your information, the meeting has been canceled. What a good news".

"For your information!?" I couldn't believe it. "I thought you were mad at me because I was making so many questions".

"And why did you think that?" he asked.

"You were typing FYI, the whole time, and I thought it meant something else".

"What exactly?"

"Fuck You Idiot"

He started laughing while I was standing there, wondering how I could think such a thing about him. I was really embarrassed and he tried to make it easier for me: "Come on, let's go for lunch, it's already late".

It wasn't yet noon and it seemed too late for him. BC At this time, in Spain there are people who hasn't still woke up" I said. Without doubt I should yet get used to these new schedules.

Occasionally, I wrote Corbalán to tell him about my experiences in Vorarlberg. He mostly replied in a funny tone but from time to time he couldn't resist a touch of drama.

Of course, his advices were priceless to me and sometimes he gave some clues about what was about to come. His experience gave him an advantage since he had gone through similar situations years ago.

In one of his answers, he explicitly asked me if I had gone already to get a haircut. According to his calculations, I should need one already. I had never considered that as something difficult to do in Austria, but again, the experience of Corbalán showed superior to my intuition.

Corbalán was indeed right, I already needed a haircut. I went to the first hairdresser I found in the city. I could hardly explain that I didn't want anything strange, just regular, short haircut.

The girl asked me how short I wanted it and I remembered that in Spain I always cut it "at number three" but I didn't know exactly what was the meaning of that number. Anyway I told myself: "numbers are just numbers, here and in Spain".

We started talking while she was cutting my hair. She was asking me about the situation in Spain, the differences that I have found so far, she looked interested on that. I asked her if she had ever been in Spain and she replied: "no, never, but once I traveled to Mexico, which is basically the same, isn't it?".

I wanted to explain to her that such an affirmation was like comparing an Austria with Germany but I didn't want her to feel bad. So I said "Well, it could be, we have some things in common".

Immersed into the conversation, I wasn't paying attention to the mirror and meanwhile the girl handled the scissors quickly, up and down. Until I realized that something was wrong, very wrong.

She saw my expression and stopped immediately. She asked me what was going on and I explained to her as best as I could that she was cutting too much.

She tried to fix it but there were almost nothing she could do at that point. After some further discussion, I finally understood that even the numbers were not the same here. In Spain they meant millimeters and in Austria the number of the machine, in a nutshell, I got a haircut 3 times shorter than I expected.

She finished her job while I tried to hold my composure. Before I left she tried to cheer me up: "don't worry, that haircut is quite popular in Mexico, is really fancy".

In order to let off steam, I told Corbalán. I was angry at him because he knew this could happen and didn't warm me. However, far from apologizing, he tried to convince me that I could still get something positive from that situation if I was determined enough to.

His answer was brief but explicit: "It doesn't matter what happens to you but. What matters is what you do about it. So the question is, what are you going to do about it, how are you going to take advantage of this?".

I could only think of how embarrassed I would be next day at the office. And during the following weeks, till the hair would grow back again. I thought a lot about that but the word resignation was emerging always in my mind. The only way out I could see was wearing my Austrian cap as long as possible.

But next day I woke up with a different mentality, from resignation courage was born, I didn't want to hide. Corbalán always said what he said for some reason, that I had already learned.

If there was something positive to get from all that, I really wanted to know what it was.

I took the train to go to work and I met Barnie there. He looked at me a few times but didn't comment on my haircut. We started talking and there was a girl in front of us, staring at us.

My friend received a phone call and while he was answering, the girl continued staring at me, smiling, like trying to find an explanation for such an exotic haircut.

"Obviously, you have questions" I told her.

She laugh and said: "Oh, sorry, I was just listening to you, you're not from here, right?".

"Ah, I thought you were impressed by my haircut".

"Well, that too".

"You know, is the latest fashion trend in Mexico, I want to spread it in Vorarlberg" I explained seriously.

We continue talking and that Austrian girl told me that next summer she would work in the same company I was worked. Apparently, she wanted to start college next year so she needed as much money as she could get.

That determination made me reflect on my progress over the last weeks. Things were going well, yes, but perhaps it was not enough to deal with problems as soon as they come up. Maybe I should go on the attack, anticipate them. I needed a new strategy.

3 Strategy

At that time, my biggest problem was the language. It was very complicated to learn. In addition, almost everyone in Vorarlberg spoke English, so I hadn't a real urgency to learn the language.

It was one of the things that surprised me when I got to Austria, many people spoke English, not only young but also older people. And nobody showed any embarrassment when talking to a stranger, in a language different from his mother tongue.

In Spain, in a similar situation, people would wait for the slightest mistake to make a joke. And if there were no error, anything that sounds funny would turn into an excuse to bring out the brave one and clog our own complexes.

My generation grow up in this kind of environment, at least regarding to languages. And that has consequences. Many began to speak English properly only once they left Spain and were force to express themselves in another language.

But learning German is even more difficult. In terms of complexity, English is simpler than the Spanish, especially the grammar. With

German happens the opposite, it's more complex and it's full of exceptions. The same with the vocabulary.

The reality is that when a person has spent years studying a simpler language, learning a more complex language becomes really complicated. That's the conclusion I came to.

Some Spaniards, also newcomers, were convinced that learning a language, whatever it was, had to be the same as learning English. Because that was the experience they had, that was what they knew and what they had lived.

So if they found more difficulties than they expected, they concluded that there must be another reasons for that. Add to that the amount of dialects in the area and our view that the Austrians were not as open as the Spaniards. Everything together formed the perfect excuse for many to justify their problems with the language.

Soon after I started working, the company offered us free German lessons. A great gesture from them. Beyond its practical use, I thought it was something to be thankful for. The rest of my colleagues didn't see it that way, they were merely complaining about the lack of quality of classes.

My answer to that was always the same: "if you don't like them, don't go, just quit, find a private academy or a private teacher". There were options, we knew a couple of good teachers in the area and an academy where students were quite satisfied.

However, nobody quit those classes. It was then when I began to understand how easy it was for some just complaining and how much satisfaction they got from that. It was his safety valve. One way to let off steam and avoid facing their problems. I understood that they would not give it up just like that.

Going back to dialects, so far all what I had learned on my own was high German. I knew that local dialects knew but didn't give them the importance that they really had, I learned that later. I thought there would be small differences, like among Spanish from different parts of Spain or South America. But it wasn't so, two Austrians in their respective dialects could literally not understand each other at all.

I went to the first German class and soon I found myself immersed in conflicts that nowadays I see as childish issues. The teacher, native, expressed herself both in dialect and in high German. For her, they were both valid and interchangeable. But for us, at that time, it was a source of misunderstandings.

I asked again and again how certain words must be pronounced and she gave me a different version each time. I got on my nerves. I had nothing against it. From the first moment I understood that she was just simply doing her job as she was told to do it.

Our relationship wasn't improving. I was quickly identified as the rebel student, and as long we knew each other better, our roles became clearer. She saw me as impertinent student and I saw her as the non devoted teacher, just doing her job for the paycheck.

Students from other groups had also complained and it was decided to conduct a survey to find out the roots of the problems. At the end of class, the teacher gave us the survey while she explained that it was important that we would provide honest answers and based on solid arguments.

She was looking directly at me as she spoke. From their point of view, my complains were not honest, neither well justified.

We left the classroom and while we were reading the questions, the group started to discuss and share opinions. Even the most shy ones were then joining the complains. I didn't agree on all of the points exposed by them, but yes on many. As I was told to do, I answered my survey honestly and based on reasons that they seemed logical to me.

This time there would be no place for misunderstanding. If all we complained more or less about the same things, they would have to correct them. We delivered the surveys, and came back next week expecting the announcement of the new measures. Nothing could be further from the truth, for the teacher everything was almost fine.

And she had reasons to see it that way. Only one student had complained about the methods, the rest had only mentioned the difficulties associated to the language but nothing about the method itself.

I couldn't believe what I was hearing. I looked at the rest of the group, asking for explanations but the shame forced most of them to bow their heads.

While the teacher was talking, I told them: "If this is only bad for me, no problem, I just quit. You complain a lot, but when you have the opportunity to change something, you just hold back. Please don't count on me for that".

I translated that to the teacher as I could and she finally persuaded me for me to stay until the end of the class so I could test the new measures she wanted to try. The truth is that at that point, I was just angry and disappointed with the rest of the group, not with her.

The teacher decided to try a new type of exercise on me, claiming that it was so easy that even me, with my lack of interest, could complete it successfully. That affirmation made me really angry.

He showed me a picture of two bedrooms, a very neat one with a mat at the door that read Silke, and another one, messy with a mat that read Petra.

"Jose, now it's your turn, look closely at this picture and tell me what you see".

I watched carefully at the picture for a couple of minutes. The teacher said: "don't you have anything to say?".

"It's just... I don't know if I can explain it correctly..".

"Come on, it's very easy".

"I don't think that it's so easy".

"Why not, what's the problem?, what don't you understand?".

"Well, I think that Petra became pregnant but it was Silke's fault, because she is an awful friend".

And there was just silence in the class. Some looked at me, doubting if I was serious or just joking. The teacher also doubted, but still encouraged me to continue:

"Look at the room of Petra, very messy, maybe a robbery? I don't think so, her skirt is on the carpet and there are a pair of man trousers on the bed. In addition, three empty bottles and some shot glasses lie on the floor".

"I think Petra went out to party, met a guy and took him to her place to go o with the party. But among so much chaos, look, there are books and papers all over the room, something was Petra looking for and couldn't certainly fin. Given the mentioned scenario, it was probably condoms".

After a brief pause, I continued: "But as I said, there are three empty bottles, too much even for a guy so at least one was drunk by Petra. More than enough to loose her wits and, eventually, stop searching for and finally making a mistake".

To my surprise, one of my colleagues was following the story and said: "okay, Petra made a mistake and became pregnant, but what that have to do with Silke?, why is all of this her fault?".

"Well, Petra and Silke are neighbors, they live alone because that's what the mats say. They are young, perhaps students, so most likely they go out together. If you take a closer look to the rooms, you can see that Petra's is large, has room for training, aerobics, yoga, whatever. But Silke's is not, is very small, she would spend all day long sitting in front of the computer. If that is so, one could say that Petra is very attractive and Silke perhaps not" I replied.

"Now imagine that they're going out together. Night after night all the guys talk to Petra and ignore Silke. She is angry about that, of course, so eventually she would say to Petra: "let's go home it's late". And Petra, sooner or later would get sick of that till the day that she decides to stay and Silke leaves alone. So that night, finally free, and containing so much accumulated desire, she ends up making the biggest mistake of her life. All because of Silke".

After that explanation, the rest of the class was astonished and we all knew that I would quit that group to never come back.

The teacher and I were not compatible and the best for all of us was, me quitting and searching for another way to learn the language, a method that really worked to me.

I sent an email to Corbalán explaining what had happened and the story about Petra and Silke. He recommended me to explain everything to my boss. He knew that I could learn by myself, but also warned me that I would have to work really hard to achieve it.

Then I must find a way to learn German, with which I felt comfortable and which allowed my team to see that I was progressing and taking that seriously.

I talked to them, I explained my reasons and when everything was clear, told them the story of Silke, to improve the atmosphere. It seemed to them the right decision and offered me some help, like starting talking to me in German, slowly and easily so I could get into the language faster.

Meanwhile, I continued searching for a method that worked for me. Barnie invited me to watch tv shows and movies in German, of course with subtitles. I had already tried in the past, when I was learning English, and I remembered that it had worked pretty well so I agreed.

Barnie was preparing a movie marathon for the weekend, with the theme of detectives, a genre that fascinated both, he and me. He invited me and some other friends, he proposed to activate the subtitles, mainly for me, and everyone accepted.

At first, I told him I was a little reluctant to marathons, I had some experiences in the past, they were funny but I doubt that they contributed so much to my mental health. Let's say that I had some ease to empathize with the characters of the series.

Once the day came, I went to his place and introduced myself to his friends. With the best of my intentions, since I was the only foreigner there, I decided to do something to break the ice.

All people there, we had two things in common, we knewBarnie and we were fans of the detective series. While the temptation of talking about Barnie and his peculiarities was huge, I thought it wasn't the best option because, in essence, he was the one who had organized that event. It wouldn't have been fair at all.

There wasn't much more time for chatting, Barnie announced the start of the marathon and we all sat around the television. I don't remember how many hours we were there. We stopped when we realized that it was late and some of us, in few hours, would have to go back to work.

When I left Barnie's place, I was aware that, once again, I had empathized too much with the character of the series. As I was walking I was making deductions about the footprints that I saw on the snow: "small dog footprints, beside female footprints heels, short distance among them so they walked fast, maybe young woman... I got it, the neighbor of Barnie has a new dog, a small one".

I went to the office the next day and i found a surprise on my desk. Someone had corrected my German notes. It would have been easy just asking who had done it, but the great detectives would never do that, he always make deductions to finally figure out who is the guilty one.

After a while analyzing clues and theories, I had a possible suspect, Doris. Doris worked with us, she was involved in all discussions and she had always something to say. She was always right. I decided to interrogate her so I text her:

"Hello, good morning Suspect #1".

"Suspect #1?, what is that?" she replied.

"Nothing look, I have a couple of questions for you".

"Ok, tell me".

"Where were you yesterday afternoon between 16:00 and 20:00?, was someone with you or you were alone?"

"Excuse me, that's none of your business"

"Yes, I know, look, the thing is that someone has corrected my notes, and all evidence point towards you".

"Sorry but it wasn't me. Why do you think that?".

"Several reasons. First, it's female handwriting, careful, delicate, no smudges or strong strokes typical from a man. Second, it must be someone who knows that I keep German notes on my desk, someone that pass often by my office. That limits the possible candidates. Third, she has used a blue marker to write, most of us we use only black markers".

"As I've said, it wasn't me. Now, leave me alone, please".

"Tell me just one thing, what color are the markers you guys use?"

"Leave me alone".

"I knew it, it was you".

"It wasn't, goodbye".

Doris didn't talk to me again for a while, neither gave me the chance to thank her for the corrections. Anyway, I knew that the detective momentum would last still some hours so I decide taking advantage of it, maybe I could use it to solve my German problem, the final problem, what to do to learn German as fast as possible.

I realized I needed someone to which explain the case, get feedback, so I could approach it from a different perspective.

My first choice was Barnie, but I already knew his opinion about that, he would say that I wouldn't be able to learn by myself so the best option would be going back to the lessons. So I decided to try Corbalán, I email him asking for advice and ideas on how to address my problem.

I waited for his response but nothing happened. Meanwhile, I received a call from Human Resources: "Jose, it's time". I was expecting that moment never to come. But it did. I had to do something that I had been avoiding during the past few weeks and I couldn't postpone it any longer.

I had to go to the bank in order to open an account, till then I was using an old Spanish account. The company had accepted that but only temporarily.

Although aware of the difficulty of the task, I tried to encourage myself and stay positive. It was a perfect occasion to consult Corbalán again but this time, I wanted to solve my problems without his help. So I answered to Human Resources: "I will go tomorrow to the bank without fail".

In theory, opening a bank account in Austria shouldn't have major complications. An on-line application must be filled, some papers must be signed and finally brought to the bank. That's all. But it can get complicated if the bank in ruled by Lady Bank A woman with two faces. An endearing grandmother in her daily life, always smiling, kind. A beast without mercy during her work shift. Every morning she went early to the bank, changed his round glasses and knit jacket for her war uniform: pointed glasses, suit and a look that would make the bravest tremble. Ready for battle. I arrived at the bank hoping to find the beloved grandmother but only the beast was there. I left willing to warn the whole world that if they wanted to survive to Lady Bank, there were three fundamental laws everyone should take into account:

First law:Lady Bank doesn't appreciate punctuality.

This is an easy one, if the bank opens at 8:00 AM, you should never arrive at 8:00 AM. I got there so punctual, that the bank was open but no one was in the cash desk. After few minutes Lady Bank showed up with a cup of coffee in one hand and a bag of muffins in the other. I had simply ruined her breakfast.

Second law:Lady Bank is always right.

I addressed her in English:"Good morning dear lady'

"Nein, no good morning. Guten Morgen" she replied in German.

I showed her my papers while she kept talking to me in German. I tried to explain her that I couldn't understand, that I could only speak English but she just simply answered: "Ok, no problem" and kept talking to me in German. There was, indeed, no problem for her.

Third law:Lady Bank never gets tired.

We were stuck in an infinite loop, I wasn't able to explain what I needed in German, neither she wanted to make the effort to understand me in English.

So there was only one option left for me, to accept the defeat and make an act of faith. I handed the papers to her and left the bank, hoping that Lady Bank would do the paperwork for me.

A week later, I found out that she had done his part and I finally had a bank account in Austria. This was certainly one of the great achievements of those times. I told Corbalán but I didn't get any response. I was surprised, Corbalán always answered fast to my emails.

Few days later, I received an email from a strange email address: "francis.thepope.theArgentinianOne@gmail.com". Few weeks ago, a new pope had been elected. It was all over the media because he was the first non-European pope. There was no reason that justify such a public figure contacting me. The message stated as follows:

Dear Jose:

This is Pope Francisco (aka Jesus Christ II), humble servant of God. Your German teacher had communicated us that you have manipulated the story of Petra and Silke. I've decided to take over this issue and expose to you the list of your faults and sins:

- *Remember the fourth commandment: "Honor your father and your mother and specially your German teacher". If he says that the exercise is easy, then easy it is. Do not look for alternative explanations. It's bad taste to challenge to authority, that makes baby Jesus cry.*

- *Petra wasn't a libertine neither had a messy bedroom. The truth is that she was working at a social center. Even she didn't have enough space to house the homeless, she was such a good Christian that she sheltered many, hence the mess.*

- *By divine will, and only for that, the love between Petra and one of the homeless emerged, and it was also divine that she couldn't find a condom. The church makes it clear, marriage or anything. Everything else is wrong, sin, hell, you should know that by now.*

- *And not only that but you dare to defame poor Silke?, a simple catechists teacher who has never hurt a fly. Silke is a saint.*

Sincerely, Francis, the Pope, the Argentinian one.

I could just write back to Corbalán and thank him for making my day. I wanted to share the story with the rest of the group, but all conversations revolved around the building of the house of one of them, materials, insulation, etc. He had brought a cake to celebrate the beginning of the construction .

That was something that seemed very interesting to me. Getting married, having a child, building a house, all was celebrated in the same way from my point of view.

Of course I was aware that in the innermost circles everything was celebrated as deserved, but from my perspective, the one of the newcomer foreign who only only had seen this kind of celebration, it seemed that they gave the same importance to everything.

The protocol was always the same. One brought a cake to the rest of the team. A cake baked by his wife. Or his bride. Or his mother ultimately. In a few months, I learned to distinguish what was being celebrated just by asking who had made the cake.

Barnie didn't think that such a deduction was possible, so I explained to him my theory:"You're married but the cake was baked by your mother?, It means you just had a son. The cake was baked by your mother and yo don't have a girlfriend?, It means you just finished the studies. You live with your girlfriend and she baked a cake?, It means the construction of your house is imminent".

It was interesting to note the paradox, the guys loved cakes a lot but they didn't want to learn to back, even more, they were proud of it. There was a typical conversation constantly repeated when someone brought a cake:

"It taste really good, did you bake it?"

"Yes".

"Come on, seriously, was it you?"

"Yes, but I got with some help".

"From your mother/ wife/ girlfriend?".

"Yes".

"So what exactly did you do?".

"Just what she told me to do".

After that break, I was still thinking about what had happened in the bank. Even though my colleagues had found the anecdote funny, I kept thinking about why it didn't work as good as I expected.

I thought I was enough good prepared, I had studied the vocabulary, prepared some phrases and typical scenarios but when the moment of truth came, I found myself blocked in front of Lady Bank. I just simply he couldn't find the words to speak my mind.

My team, supportive as always, try to cheer me up by explaining to me that that experience had been actually positive and it would help me in the future "it's just another stepping stone" they said. But my sole conclusion was that I should spend more time and effort learning German. What I had done so far, wasn't enough.

The weekend was just around the corner and the weather forecast not good so I plan an intense plan to improve my German, convinced that this time, once and for all, I would improve substantially and the days of misunderstanding and troubles would become just memories of a difficult beginning.

After several hours studying, I decided to take a break and watch a movie in German. I tried first without subtitles. Big mistake. Several minutes passed and I had understood anything. I activated the subtitles, but it didn't improve too much, I wasn't still able to follow the plot.

I decided to try something easier, Spanish audio and German subtitles. Again big mistake. I was so focused on the film that I was ignoring the subtitles.

I turn the TV on for a while and it was when I had a moment of perfect clarity. A Star Wars movie was about to start and as the result of fatigue an idea came to my mind: "my big problem is just the grammar, the words order so different than in Spanish. But that's how Yoda speaks, he changes the order of the words, so that means tha Yoda, in German, will be easier for me to understand".

And that's the problem of not having proper resting, it may cloud reason and judgment. An idea like that can seem a really good one.

I started watching the movie, anxious to listen to Yoda and begin to, finally, understand German. It took several minutes but eventually he appeared and started talking. The order of words was different, that's true, but I couldn't still understand so much. It didn't take me long to realize how brilliant my idea was.

For the coming week, I decided to try different strategy. Based on music and listening to local radio, to motivate and immerse myself in the language.

The motivation part was important because at that time I was a bit depressed. I was having troublse getting used to the lack of light. In Austria it gets dark earlier than in Spain, of course, but I wasn't still used to the 5 PM sunsets.

Besides, I started early in the morning to work what it meant that during several weeks I was going to work and coming back home in the darkness. I didn't see daylight at all. That's why it was so important to keep motivation as high as possible.

On Monday morning, loaded with music, I took the train to the office. I was listening to some rock music that reminded me the last summer holidays in Spain. I was so absorbed by those memories that I missed my stop and had to catch an additional train.

I arrived later than expected to the office, still listening to my music, when I saw that there were some operators working in the workarounds of the building entry. It wasn't yet daylight so I tried to stay away from the trees, covered by snow and waiting I was close enough to release their load. I was so focused that I missed the only puddle in the area and stomp in, with the bad luck that it was also icy, slipped and fell down.

It wasn't the best way to start the week, no doubt. I thought that there was always the option of investing more time, keep pushing, but I knew deep down that wasn't the best way.

At noon I had lunch with Barnie. He was strangely radiant but he said nothing about it. My attempts to get information were in vain. He was still smiling, aware that he was hiding a very juicy secret. It was clear to me that something good had happened to him during the weekend.

I abandoned the interrogation, sure that sooner or later he couldn't hold it anymore and he would tell me. Barnie tried to lead the conversation, I was aware of that. He was asking what I had done during the weekend, how I was doing with girls and so on.

So I asked him about his weekend and his pride was stronger than him and finally me his story.

He had gone out with his friends and, as usual, spent most of the night drinking and theorizing about women, which pickup lines worked best, etc.

Withinn that group Barnie felt superior, and possibly he was. His lack of skills were compensated by his courage and bravery, which sometimes allowed him to succeed in situations in which none of his friends could ever have.

Immersed in the discussion with his friends, a girl approached him asking to take a photo of her and her friends. Barnie observant as always, noticed that the girl's accent was foreign and started talking to her.

It turned out that the girl was part of our Spanish group. From the information that Barnie gave me, I was almost sure to know who she was. She lived with her boyfriend in Vorarlberg, I felt tempted to tell Barnie but then I realized that it would be more fun not to tell him and let him continue with his story.

After taken the picture, Barnie seized his chance and kept talking with the girl, developing all his Spanish abilities. His friends looked at him amazed.

Nothing happened that night, Barnie offered to help her with the German and practicing some Spanish as well. Although it was clear that his intentions were others.

The girl, already used to these kind of situations, found an elegant way out, without Barnie noticing it at all. He asked her for her number, email, but she convinced him that it wasn't necessary, she always went to that bar so they would meet there often and could continue practicing.

What Barnie didn't know is that that was an exception, the entire group went out to celebrate a birthday. The girl wasn't a big fan of that type of clubs. But who was I to remove the illusion from my friend Barnie. He looked so happy.

We went back to work and the excitement of Barnie became heavier. It didn't matter that we were talking about, everything revolved around to end in the same topic, how well he had done with the girl, how good he was with women in general.

At first I ignored him, but in order to keep my attention he took it to a personal level, he started comparing us and feeling sorry that I wasn't so skillful as he. Moreover, he stated that Spaniards were not able to talk to the girls in Vorarlberg as he did. None of us had the gifts he had.

It was of course his opinion, quite far from reality, but I didn't feel strong enough to keep discussing. Even though, that was irritating me, and I started to feel how my motivation grew with each passing moment.

It was then when I had the idea that would change completely the course of the following weeks. I could do better than him, much better. Barnie had practiced Spanish one day with a girl. I could do better than that, so I decided to focus my efforts in German conversations, in doing tandems with girls also interested in speaking Spanish.

Being aware that I could do it, it seemed to me like a great opportunity, I would close his mouth once and for all and my German would improve dramatically.

I started with easy steps. I knew a girl in Human Resources who spoke a bit Spanish so I explained to her my idea and she liked it. She was just starting with the language and she was really nice so it seemed to me a good candidate to try the tandem approach.

We started meeting once a week and talked during half an hour more or less. And it went well, for both of us. It wasn't long until Barnie noted us, and he interrogated me about it, I just kept my answers and explanations to the minimum expression. What, by the way, made that situation even more intriguing for him.

I was gradually widening my tandem circle. I reached four tandems up and running and began to have problems to keep all of them running at the same time. I couldn't always find time for all of them.

In addition, the topics of the conversations were very different so I had to remember with who I had already talked about what and so on.

The good news was that during those months my German improved drastically. I wasn't speaking good yet, but surely more fluid. I realized I could use what I knew, what it was a great step forward.

As expected, the news was spread quickly in the company and there was a rumor about a Spanish guy who had learned German just by talking to girls. Nothing else.

Precisely that was what I didn't want, fame and expectations. I was happy with my progress but still needed lots of improvement, it seemed unfair that fame that I was given.

My great fear was concerning Barnie and the rest of Spanish people. Even though it was his attitude and opinions what had motivated me to go on and achieve what he said I couldn't, I didn't feel good about it. I neither liked the implied comparisons that the rest of the Spanish people in the company would have to suffer.

Some started asking me about the effectiveness of the tandems, if it was true that they really worked, and even Rafa, one of the Spaniards of the company, was motivated to try one. It was working for him at the beginning but after a while, it diluted, in my opinion because none of them have a strong enough reason to go on.

The rest of the group didn't have changed their minds, the discussion topics remained the same, that surprised me a lot. Even with an example like mine on the table, showing that it was possible to integrate with the people here, learn the language, talk to them, etc. They kept stating that it was not possible.

At first I decided to avoid those discussions, I couldn't get anything positive from them. I desisted even from helping them, it was clear to me that they were not interested in finding a solution to the problem, just using it to justify themselves and ultimately protect their self-esteem.

4 Spanish connection

During the first months in Austria I was living in a hotel, courtesy of the company. Since the beginning, they supported me to find an apartment but it wasn't easy, there were few flats and empty rooms available. My intention was to share a flat with German or Austrian people, in order to integrate as fast as possible.

I also had the option of renting an apartment for myself, but I didn't like the idea. Sharing a flat with Spaniards also possible, but I had discarded that idea, I wanted to put myself into an uncomfortable environment sort of speak.

Few weeks later, I found a room in an apartment where they were living two Germans guys, more or less my age, football fans like me. I liked it and decided to take it. The same week that FC Barcelona and FC Bayern Munich were playing together, I move to the flat. My new flat mates asked me to watch the game with them but I wasn't really attracted by the idea. At that time, Bayern was playing far better than Barcelona so it didn't seem to me funny at all.

But they insisted and finally convinced me to join them. I came home after work and found them, both on the sofa, wearing the shirt of Müller and Schweinsteiger respectively, drinking beers and with war paint on theirs faces. They were ready for battle.

I sat between them and in few minutes the game was already on. As expected, Bayern was playing much better. It was only a matter of time Bayern would score the first goal, I knew it, my flat mates knew it.

After an elaborated play, Müller appeared in the penalty area and scored. They looked at me doubtfully, they didn't know whether celebrate the goal or respect my pain. Anyway, they tried to cheer me up "It was clearly offside, what a referee" they said.

During the second half, I made up thousand of excuses to escape from there, like "I have to call my family", "I have to send a mail to my boss ", but each time I returned to the sofa, the show was worse and worse, 2-0, 3-0, one guy had waving his Bayern scarf, the other was complaining in German because there were no more cold beers.

I was in my room when Bayern scored the fourth goal of the night, I heard it but my flat mates were not celebrating this time, just whispering between them. One of them came to my room and said: "You don't want to see the rest of the game...".

"Oh yes, of course, I go in a moment".

"No, no, I mean that "you don't want to see the rest of the game" trust me".

"What happened?"

"Let's say that... *Debakle* could be the word of the day".

"4-0??"

"Yeahhh!! Oh my god what a goal from Müller! you've should seen it! what an amazing player!"

"Ok, I see..".

"But hey... don't worry, I'm sure that Barcelona will win the next game".

Even though, sharing an apartment with them was nice. They didn't socialize as much as the Spaniards, but we had a good time, even some weekends we went out together and had good times.

One of them found a job in his country and announced us that he would leave the flat in a couple of weeks. He called the landlord to tell him and that same day he came to visit us, to explain us that he already had a candidate for the free room. His company had hired a Spanish guy, who would arrived to Vorarlberg in a couple of weeks.

That sounded good to us, especially to me because the new guy came from southern Spain, an area where people are really charming and have a great sense of humor. The landlord had told him that there was already a Spaniard leaving in the flat, so he was very excited to start living with us.

The same day that the German guy left, the new Spaniard was moving to the flat, so we decided to prepare something for dinner in order to welcome him warmly.

From the balcony, my flatmate and me saw the new guy arriving, he was driving his van with the side windows down and the music really loud. He was listening flamenco and singing like crazy. I told my colleague:"Here comes Flamenquito, the new guy" but he didn't get the joke.

The German was carrying his stuff in the car andFlamenquito parked beside him. With that art and grace that characterizes the people of the south, he spoke to the German guy in Spanish, thinking it was me: "Illo what's up! I'm finally here!"but the German guy couldn't understand anything.

"Ohu illo, tell me something! insisted Flamenquito, but the German was just staring at him, thinking "who is this guy?, Is he trying to steal from me?, and why is he screaming so much?".

"Uy uy uy, well don't worry, after a couple of beers you will start talking, you'll see".

I went out to save the German guy and introduce myself. As expected, we were talking all night long, sharing experiences and opinions. We lost the notion of time, we weren't aware that the next day we had to go to work.

I told him about the differences I'd seen so far between Austria and Spain, like the hours related, the stores were closed earlier than in Spain, people had lunch and dinner earlier and of course they woke up much earlier. "Most of the people is awake and ready to work at 6AM" I told him.

It got so late that the next morning I struggled like never before with the alarm clock. I went down to the kitchen to have breakfast, more asleep than awake, and when entering into the kitchen I had the feeling that something was wrong, something was going on but I didn't know exactly what.

"Maybe I'm just tired after last night" I told myself. I sat down and started having breakfast when suddenly something called my attention. The clock on the wall was literally spinning out of control, the hands were rotating really fast.

Even I knew I wasn't in my best condition, I tried to find a logical explanation for what I was seeing:

- It could be a joke of Flamenquito.
- It could be that the clock is not working properly anymore.
- Or perhaps it's a paranormal phenomenon.

But, just when I was sure that the clock was broken, it returned to its normal speed, I couldn't explain that, it didn't seem like a failure. I kept looking at it and few seconds after later it started again to turn like crazy.

So the question was, what could I do in such a situation? Should I destroy it, run away from it, hide under the table?. I chose an easy path, I finished my breakfast and recorded everything with my handy so I could proof in the future what I was just witnessing.

I went to work and explained to Barnie what happened. To my surprise, it turns out that there was a simple explanation for that. In Austria, wall clocks are "radio-controlled", which means that they synchronize themselves with a time radio signal. It was the first time that I saw something like that. The clock was simply synchronizing itself.

So Barnie, still puzzled, asked me: "What did you think it was happening?".

"Well...I had some theories".

"Any of them reasonable?"

"Well... reasonable, reasonable, maybe not".

During the rest of the week, my German colleague and me were getting to know Flamenquito. He worked hard, he came home really late each afternoon, tired, but always talking about going out during the weekend.

We didn't know so many people in the area, but the German guy was living here longer and had more friends. Therefore, he invited us to a small party in the place of an Austrian friend.

Flamenquito was excited with the plan, after a long working week, he needed to go out and clear his mind. We got there and the Austrian guy greeted us warmly: "Hallo, how are you? please come in ". Flamenquito, tried to enter the house without taking his shoes off.

"*Nein nein*,Flamenquito, you have to take your shoes off".

"Illo but how am I going to walk barefoot, it's so cold!"

"Well, it's an Austrian tradition".

"Ah, Austrian tradition. Ok then" said Flamenquito while taking his shoes off slowly.

"Look, this is and Andalusian tradition. Ole!, ole!, ole!" said while he began to dance in front of the Austrian guy.

The guy, far from being frightened, was enjoining the show and started clapping and yelling to Flamenquito"Ole!, ole!".

Finally we walked in and sat down to have some cake and a chat a bit. Few minutes later, Flamenquito was already bored, he wanted to go out, explore the bars of the area, but the people wanted to stay there, calmed and relaxed.

He grabbed his handy and started looking for options. He found a the facebook group, named "Spaniards in Vorarlberg" and asked about places to go out and people interested on hanging out. One Spaniard answered him. he said they were celebrating a birthday party and we could join them if we wanted to.

In less than an hour, Flamenquito and me were already at the party, integrating in that new group of Spaniards.

There were about 20 people there, most of them from south Spain, lot of wine, Spanish food and music. Finally Flamenquito had found his place. A couple of hours later, I saw Flamenquito wandering into the living room, concentrated, looking at the floor, as he was searching for something:

"Illo what's up?"

"Nothing illo, I was thinking about something".

"Ok, about what?" I asked.

"Look, the fact is that I've never understood why there were so many kind of socks, you know, colors, shapes and so on".

"But now, look around, we are all barefoot".

"Check that out, some are striped, other have square shapes. They all look really nice".

"So?"

"So now it all makes sense, don't you see it? Socks are meant to be to show off. Because we are barefoot the whole night".

"Life is crazy, right?" I said

"Yes it is, my friend, yes indeed " he replied.

We kept talking all night long and he told me about the problems he had with the German, it was very difficult for him to learn the language. I explained him what I was doing with tandems, but time wasn't convinced enough to give it a try.

At that time, my tandems were working properly, Flamenquito was an endless source of stories. My partners found them very funny, and the fact that I was repeating the same stories over and over helped me a lot to improve. Before Flamenquito era, I had troubles speaking every day with a different partner, finding topics to talk about, but now it seemed to me that everything was simpler.

By repeating the same stories so many times, it wasn't only easier to express myself better in German, but I was learning to identify which parts of the language I found more difficult. Of course not all tandems went well, it was really difficult to find the perfect partner for such an activity.

For example, some tried to talk the least possible in Spanish because they didn't feel still comfortable enough, which afterwards I realized, I was encouraging unconsciously by turning those conversations into monologues about Flamenquitoand his adventures.

Another girl switched to English almost all the time, she was more interested in socializing than practicing the language. I had always thought that these kind of situations were more typical with a guy proposing a tandem to a girl and having other intentions in mind. It seemed I was wrong.

There was only a tandem that was working so good that I could really see it lasting long in future. My partner was an Austrian girl who could speak Spanish pretty well.

There were two things that made that tandem so special and effective. First, we got along pretty well and second, we both care about that the other spoke enough in the language he was learning.

We had no rules, no turns, no predetermined topics. We just began to talk in German or Spanish indistinctly and when one decided to change, the other trusted that it wasn't a selfish action. The amount of time that we dedicated to each language was normally the same.

Of course, there were times when we used more one language than another, perhaps days in which we spoke mostly English. But I think it was understandable, after all this was just another kind of relationship between two people, in which not always both are in best possible shape.

There were days that I would pay to avoid speaking German, others instead I wanted desperately to talk as much as possible. And for her it was the same.

I had more opportunities to speak German, mainly because of the change of residence and having a German flatmate, so I decided to focus only in the tandem that was working really good. And with the rest I just put them aside, I kept meeting the other partners but less often until we decided to leave it.

Now, with more free time, Flamenquito and I started meeting more often the Spanish group. They were all working in Vorarlberg. A group of around 50 members, nice people, different ages but mostly young. Some of them were leaving in Austria for several years, most of them were sporty and all of them without exception, crazy about going out and having parties.

I realized that all conversations, predictably, were focused on the cultural differences, the language, etc. There were a small group really pessimistic when it comes to our integration in Vorarlberg. They thought that it was just impossible. And it's curious, because they were the same that they did little or no effort to integrate at all.

The main topic was always the dialect, "an impossible challenge" they said, not even to speak it but to understand it. It was clear for me that I didn't want to participate in such a discussion. I was the new guy, and knowing us as I do, I knew for sure that my optimism would be perceived as arrogance and pride.

I have to admit that during those early days, I got carried away by pessimism and one day, I behave like them. I had decided to explore the surroundings of my neighborhood and had found a bakery close to my place.

I entered and barely could communicate with the baker. An old gentleman who didn't seem to have traveled a lot and had no sympathy for foreigners, even less when they couldn't express themselves correctly in his language. Instead of figuring out what I could do about that, I found myself thinking negatively and blaming the baker for not being nicer with me.

Next time I met with the group of Spaniards, I told them what had happened to me with the baker. It wasn't my intention just to complain but to show them that even it was difficult, it was still possible to be understood.

To my surprise, they took that as the ultimate evidence of their negative speech. That was, according to them, the irrefutable proof that there theories were correct. Integration wasn't possible. The dialect was a barrier.

I hesitated for a moment, maybe they were right, but at the same time I was really motivated by the idea to overcome this situation and prove them wrong. I had an internal conflict, I didn't like getting so motivated just by proving that I was right and they didn't.

I wrote to Corbalán, explaining him the situation and seeking for advice. He replied quickly, terse, and with some additional questions:"No matter the problem, no matter what happens to you, what matters is what are you going to do about it. What will you do to solve that problem?"

After reflecting about that for a while, I finally decided to insist until the baker would change his attitude. There were only two possible outcomes in my mind, the baker would change his attitude towards me or I would continue going to the bakery till that man would retire. There were no more options.

So the next day I went back to the bakery, with the usual problems to explain myself, but finally I got what I wanted. When I left the bakery, I shout "goodbye" effusively to the baker and stared at him, expressing my intention of going back next day.

I kept going the rest of the week, every day with a bigger smile, greeting and chatting with the rest of the people there waiting for their turn. Gradually, the baker stopped grunting every time he saw me coming, which was definitely an achievement.

Until one day, once the conversation about the bread was a piece of cake, I tried something new and said: "Today I would like that one, in Spain we don't have it and want to try it".

And then the miracle happened. The baker spoke instead of grunting: "So, you are Spanish, right?"?

"Yes, I came here to work because in my country the situation is not good.".

"Ahhh I see, I heard something about that. But at least football is still great, right?"

"Yes, in that we are one of the best".

"We too, once we beat Germany in Cordoba, almost 40 years ago".

And now he was where I wanted him to be, becoming slowly more friendly, step by step. I will always remember when, one day early in the morning, I went out jogging and past by the bakery, the baker came out and shouted me: "Spain!, I'm running out of bread, should I put one bar aside for you?"

"Yes! Thank you very much, I'll come back for it in half an hour!"

"Ok great, enjoy your running".

Thrilled with such a success, I couldn't wait to get home and write to Corbalán. I sent him an email with the whole story. He was proud of me succeeding where others had failed. I had also told him that I was thinking about sharing that story with the group of Spaniards and try to inspire them to do the same.

His response, however, was the opposite of what I was expecting. Instead of supporting my new idea, he was inviting me to not tell them. He said: "These people have their established idea, they all accept it as a group. If you go there and tell them that they all are wrong, then they will choose to discredit your story. Our Spanish pride often prevents us from acknowledge our mistakes. Find someone who can judge your story with fairness and you can be inspired by it".

And after reflecting on his words, I began to realize he was right, we are proud, perhaps selfish and arrogant. And withing that group, very few looked capable to get some benefit from my story. In fact, those who could take advantage from it where the same that no longer needed, the same that already spoke well and were comfortable living here.

Even though, I had a potential candidate, Rafa, a Spanish guy working in the same company I did, and the one who, not long ago, I was started to play table tennis with. He wasn't part of the Spanish group. He shared some of their opinions but he was smarter than most of them, he was able to listen to people instead of just complaining all the time.

He was in the company longer than me, but he wasn't so lucky as I was. His team was a very special one, in which the integration was very difficult. Most of the members were interested only in doing their jobs, not in being involved, not in worrying about the rest of the group.

In addition, the ones that should set an example and encourage another kind of behavior, were more concerned to live calm and relaxed than doing what it was supposed to be part of their responsibility.

I decided to take the risk and I told him the story. At the beginning, Rafa didn't see it clear, but letting egos aside for a moment, he finally admitted that this was the way to go. If he didn't do the same so far was simply because he wasn't interested, he liked his current life, he didn't feel the need of seeking for more.

We started talking more often and since we had a tennis table in the company, we started playing together and soon, our matches become interesting and funny. Rafa won most of the times, he simply played much better than me.

Some weeks later, matches were more level, anyone could win, and since early in the morning we run our personal psychological games, trying to discourage the other.

Rafa was very competitive, he couldn't stand losing. Whenever he was winning he smiled and made jokes the whole time. Whenever he was losing, not a word, not a joke.

It was useless trying to explain to him that it didn't matter who won, or that the important thing was to play a little bit every day, his answer was always the same "even you don't believe that".

One of those weeks, I was really on file, three victories in a row. Next day Rafa came to my office and communicated me that he couldn't play more this week, he had a lot of work.

I found that understandable, till that very that same day, late in the afternoon, I saw him playing with another guy way better than us.

I watched them for a while and I realized they were not playing, the other guy was training Rafa. They continued the rest of the week like that I decided don't tell anything to Rafa.

On Monday he came back to visit me, this time more cheerful than usual, he said: "Come on, let's go to play".

"I thought you had lots and lots of work?" I said.

"Well, yes, I had, but right now we are more relaxed".

"Okay, let's go then".

We started playing and since the beginning I realized he had improved a lot. The first jokes and smiles appeared soon. Due to the location of the table, an inner courtyard, we could be observed from many offices, even heard if doors were open we hear.

So this time we have an audience and Rafa was really enjoying. I decided then to take more risks. Whether my drives were good or bad, the result was always the same, Rafa had to go and pick up the ball wherever it had fallen. During those seconds, I pretended to celebrate the point as if I had won. He couldn't see me but the audience, from the distance, thought I was winning.

As expected, I failed more points than I won, victory for Rafa, but as soon the game was over I celebrated as if I had won. I raised my hands to the sky and people started clapping. Rafa looked at me surprised, not understanding what was happening. Until one of my teammates yelled at him: "Hey Rafa, is this always like this?, Jose always beats you?

"What are you saying, I always beat him!" replied Rafa

"Come on Rafa, we've all seen the match".

"He has no chance of beating me!"said Rafawhile becoming angrier.

"Rafa, you were the whole time picking up the ball".

"Because he missed all the points!"

"Rafa, what a bad loser!"

And Rafa looked at me, not knowing exactly what to say, but very angry: ": But you... But you..."

"But me anything" I interrupted him "you said you couldn't play because you had too much work when in fact, you were training".

Fortunately, few days later, we made peace again and started playing again, offering from time to time quite an entertaining show. Somethings would never change, I was still celebrating my fake victories when I lost and he continued with his jokes and smiles when he was winning.

Rafa had arrived to Vorarlberg one year before me. It was clear for him since the beginning that he didn't want to share a flat. He found an apartment only for him and he was comfortable living alone. The idea behind that was that his girlfriend, at that time living in Spain, would someday come and join him in Vorarlberg. So, his decision was quite understandable from my point of view.

But there were more reasons, he appreciated the silence, the peace, the pleasure of being alone at home and don't need to talk to anyone, specially after a long day full of discussions and arguments with all kind of people.

And that called my attention. I had never lived alone, in fact, I had always thought that I would be incredibly boring. But I could relate to the reasoning of Rafa , I identified myself with them.

There was another issue, the money. Of course it was cheaper to share instead of renting alone, but the impact at the end of the month wasn't so big as I had originally assumed.

I began to think that maybe it was the moment for me, to find and apartment only for me. I discussed it within the Spanish group and to my surprise, most of the people were the opinion that it was the best choice, full of advantages and with an unique drawback, the money.

In my team I got more or less the same answers, but there was one exception, Barnie, who saw any form of rent as a waste of money. The only valid option for him was to live in a home, designed and built by oneself. He talked about it, as typical in Vorarlberg, like "the project of his life".

But there was something he didn't like to tell, something that the others had already told me just by humility and coherence. It was the fact that not everyone could do that, build an own house. Many Austrian citizens couldn't afford to build a house those days.

One impediment was the ground, increasingly expensive. Without that, the vital project became almost impossible. Still, full of irony, Barnie had lived since few years in a rented apartment and still had no date to begin the construction of his palace.

So I didn't spend much time thinking about it, I knew I wanted to do it and have an apartment only for myself and I was ready to deal with the whole process. After the experiences that I had had so far, I knew it wouldn't be easy but at least interesting and funny.

5 A new beginning

Searching for a new apartment in Vorarlberg can be painful. The offer is reduce, the demand is high and most of the landlords prefer local tenants, with which they can communicated without problems. Some are still a bit skeptical about foreigners.

I wasn't lucky in my first tries to find an apartment. The first flat I went to visit, was owned by a gentleman who besides distrustful, believed he has all rights in the world to rip me off just because I was a foreigner in his country. Furthermore, he considered me an idiot since his wiles were not exactly subtle.

I think he was one of those people who have never traveled away, never left their country, or possibly its region, neither wanted to do it and possibly all they know about the rest of the world is what they see occasionally on TV or in the news.

I realized there were some differences, when looking for a flat in Austria or in Spain. Here the rent includes the water, the heating, etc. Prices are more or less similar but flats are mostly unfurnished. Of course, most landlords care about their tenants and their problems, but as usual there are always some exceptions.

So at first time I had found the exception, a man who was only interested in money and didn't want to know anything about the problems of his tenants. Now I know how easy these landlords are easy to spot. When I see in the newspaper ads that 90% of flat offers are 1-2 weeks old, and the other 10% is around 1-3 months, I understand who is who.

Anyway, I went to see the apartment, because it was in a very good location and the rent price was very reasonable.

At the meeting time, he was there, at the door waiting for me, smoking and with a grim look. We came in and he began to explain the conditions: "Before starting, you must know that the deposit is 3 months rent".

"Ok".

"Do you have money to pay for it?".

"Yes, I do". I replied surprised.

"If you want to pay now, I accept credit cards, Mastercard, Visa and American Express".

"I would like to see the rest of the apartment first, please".

"Yes, yes, of course. Here is the kitchen, the fridge is old, but for a small fee I can get you a new one".

"Does the glass-ceramic hob work well?"

"Yes, of course, but if you want, I can ask for a review and include that in your deposit".

"Wait, should I pay for that?"

"Yes! That's it!, do you want me to make a budget?"

"No, it's ok, don't worry".

"This is the living room (unfurnished), previous renters bought furniture at Ikea, but I will tell one thing, don't trust large companies, they will cheat on you. Instead, me...".

"Oh please, don't tell me you also sell furniture".

"Yes! here in my handy I have some pictures, do you want to take a look?"

"No, thanks, let's continue please".

We finished seeing the apartment and the owner continued with his speech, I could only think of how to get out of there. Suddenly he changed his tone and said: "I will tell you one thing, I can tell you love the apartment and I like you, so I will make an exception here. I will reduce the rent by 10 euros if we close the deal today. You can sign here".

And he took from his folder a contract, with my name on it, ready to be signed. I politely declined the offer and escaped from there as fast as I could.

By then Flamenquito was also looking for an apartment. We would have liked to share but he wanted to live in another part Vorarlberg so he would be closer to work. All related with Internet and computers wasn't for him, he felt more comfortable looking for flats in the newspaper.

One day, he came to my room asking for advice about an apartment: "Illo look, what do you think about this one?".

"But have you done here, you've destroyed the newspaper!, and these scribbles?" I asked.

"Well you know, I've always seen in the movies how they grab the paper and make nice circles on it, but I didn't work, I tore the paper. And I told myself, circles are not my thing, let's try an X, as in the football pools, that's very Spanish".

I went with him to see the apartment, he liked it and got it. We organized him a small farewell party and few weeks after he left, I found a flat that I really liked. It was small, with a terrace, good price and not far away from downtown.

My new landlord was also a peculiar person, an old man suspicious of foreigners, especially from the east. I was lucky to have the help of a lady from my company, friend of him, who interceded for me and finally convinced him to rent me the apartment.

With the help of Flamenquito, in less than a week I was already living on the new apartment, with the basics to survive.

The first days were not as I expected. I had in mind something like in the movies, a small community with a familiar environment, in which the different characters collide at first but eventually end up getting along and being part of a big family.

Here, each made his own life, never exceeding the minimal courtesy, just greeting. We didn't have in that building common areas where to meet occasionally with neighbors. Well, we shared the washers room, but even that wasn't enough.

I made a round through the building asking how the washing machines worked and I realized that I wouldn't make any friends there. Surely, the scriptwriters of the films had lived in other kind of neighborhoods.

But my motivation was still at maximum levels, now I was living alone, total freedom. During the weekend I just wanted to celebrate such an event. The Spanish group knew I had moved already to the new flat so they joined me in the celebration.

Nothing out of the ordinary, we went from bar to bar, collecting beers until some no longer knew what their names were. In my case, when I was already aware that I wasn't right, my biggest concern was to don't mistake my way back home and ending at the other side of the city.

My worries banished when the next beer round was poured. And after that, another one. The next thing I remember was waking up on my couch, hearing the neighbors talking among themselves.

"Well, it seems that here the walls are very thin" I thought. I could heard their voices perfectly, crystal clear. I got up from the couch, still trying to figure out why I was sleeping there and not in my bed when I heard someone going upstairs and greeting again "Good morning".

But this time, the greeting was for me. The front door was open, and on the other side a lady was looking stunned to new foreign, who had slept on the couch with the door open.

I put myself together and greeted her back as if nothing had happened there. I closed the door and went to bed. Later, in better conditions, I remembered that when I got home last night I had tried to close the door but apparently I had failed and without being aware of it, I just surrendered and lied on the sofa to get finally some sleep.

I spent the first days buying and assembling furniture. Flamenquito and Rafa helped me with the heavy work, but there were still details that were causing me major complications, such as getting the right pillow.

Used to the Spanish ones, tall, long, slightly wider and rather hard, the Austrian one didn't work for me, square, without consistency, extremely light. In the end, I had to buy one on the Internet, in a Spanish website.

The next step, supposedly easier, was to buy everything related to cleaning. At least a broom, to begin with. In the supermarket there were many, but I couldn't believe those prices.

So I decided to check in the Internet again, where I found quite a similar offer but cheaper. To be more effective, I changed the delivery address so from now on, all packets would be sent to the company.

I ordered the broom and in a few days I was supposed to receive it at the company. Usually when we get a package, the store guys send us an email letting us know where to pick it up. But this time I didn't receive any email, they called me.

"Jose, Warehouse speaking".

"Hi, what's up?"

"Look, we need you to come here as soon as possible, we received your broom and we need you to take it to make room".

"Ok I go... wait, how do you know that is a broom?"

And he put me on the speaker, I could heard them all laughing.

"Just come here, you'll see...".

And I went down to the warehouse, intrigued. From the distance I could see the guys waiting for me, phones were ready to capture the moment. And there it was, a great mistake, I had bought an outside broom, a huge one, and the packaging made it even more enormous.

When I arrived where the broom was, the party started. It was understandable, the broom was bigger than me. I took it as I could and tried to get out of there. But the guys followed me because they knew that the best was yet to come.

I had to go up two floors to get to my office, pass by Human Resources department and finally Rafa's office. I knew it, the guys knew it.

Even I was sure that the broom he wouldn't fit into the elevator, I tried. The door opened and a cleaning lady came out. While she watched amazed such as tremendous broom, she said something in German that I couldn't understand but the guys found it very funny. Of course, there was no humane way to put that monster into the elevator.

I decided to take the stairs as run as fast as possible. I got to the second floor without meeting anyone, "maybe if I made no noise, nobody in Human Resources would note me" I thought. But just around the corner, the broom swept away a pot and the whole department went out to see what was going on.

I walked decided, as if nothing happened, but the trail of paparazzi betrayed me. I kept walking till I was closed to Rafa's office. I saw he was on the phone so I had a chance to go unnoticed.

I was about to succeed when one of the guys warned Rafa, who quickly went out. He held his laughter for a moment but finally shouted at me: "hey, where you go Harry Potter?, don't forget to put on the glasses before taking off!". And I couldn't reply anything. That same afternoon, Rafa was supposed to help me bringing and assembling the latest pieces of furniture.

Few days later, the flat was almost ready. And I was exhausted. I needed to disconnect. The weather was better, first sunny days, and it surprised me how active the people was in Vorarlberg when the weather was nice, as if they wanted to squeeze every minute of sunlight.

I called Flamenquito to go out for a drink and he loved the idea. He was very stressed lately, only when we started talking about organizing a barbecue on the river, he looked happy. We had tried many times to do that but never found the perfect day for it. That weekend instead, seemed the one.

We met the rest of Spanish group in the river and few minutes the barbecue was running. The sky was clear, we took a bath, it was a great day. But after a couple of hours, the first clouds appeared, we looked at each other with some concerns. Just as we feared, in a matter of minutes it began to rain.

Among the chaos of ones complaining and others seeking shelter, Flamenquito ran away without saying a word. Before we noted it, he was back with his van and the music out loud. He parked next to the barbecue and his show began.

He unfolded an awning from one side of the van, which in happened to had two legs to fix it on the floor. "Now we can protect us from the rain"he said. He took a couple of folding chairs and the first standing ovation of the evening was for him.

Took a briefcase that no one knew what it was for, left us a few moments wondering, and with a pair of agile movements unfolded it and the case turned into a table with 4 seats. Almost as if by magic.

People were astonished, they sang, applauded him, and suddenly someone asked the hero of the afternoon to say a few words. Flamenquito accepted, he adopted a serious pose while appeased the masses. He looked at the sky... to his audience... to his van... and said: "Let it rain...".

We spent all summer having barbecues, going to river and playing football. After so many years without playing, I was enjoying it again, so I started to play regularly with some colleagues from the company. We had a football field next to our building, which made things easier.

But first things first, I needed new boots. I wen with Barnie to the store so he could help me with the translation. A very nice girl attended us, who was able to stand Barnie's jokes as I had never seen before:

"Good morning, I can help you with something?" said the girl.

"Yeah, look, my friend needs a pair football boots" answered Barnie.

"Any particular model?"

"Mmm... my friend needs ones that run really fast'.

The girl, far from being intimidated, ignored him: "Perfect, these are the ones from Cristiano Ronaldo, 200 euros".

"Not bad, which are the ones that score a lot of goals?"

"Here, Messi's ones, 200 euros also".

"Hell, very expensive. Do you have any cheaper?"

"Of course, I have these on discount, the ones that Sergio Ramos used during the final of the Confederations Cup".

"But he missed a penalty there...".

"50% discount".

"Don't say anything else. Deal".

So the next match day I went to work with my new boots in the bag, eager to start playing. I spent all morning looking at them like a kid.

An hour before the game, we received an email: "Match is canceled because gardeners are doing field maintenance". Bad luck.

Half an hour later, they sent another email: "There is a piece of field we can use and play 4 vs 4". For me that was more than enough, I just wanted to try my boots.

I went down to play, really motivated, but when I got to the field, I found the rest of the players barefoot. I couldn't understand it. They looked at me even more puzzled and said:"where you go with that, here in Austria we always play barefoot!". I couldn't believe it. I finally agreed to play barefoot, I was already there, I had nothing to lose.

But after some minutes, I was aware of my mistake. I wasn't prepared for a challenge of that magnitude. Rafa was also there and had same problems so we left as soon as we could.

We sat on the train and started talking, as usual, in Spanish, there were no reason to speak German between us, for that we had already the lessons and the tandems.

Near us, there was a girl who lived in my neighborhood, never spoke to her, but had seen enough times to know who she was and greet occasionally.

While talking to Rafa about trivial issues, I realized that the girl was staring at us. I didn't give it more importance, it wasn't the first time, we were already used to that kind of situations. We reached our destination and when leaving the train, I said goodbye to the girl to what she replied in perfect German: "You speak actually very good Spanish".

I was puzzled but thanked her and moved on. Meanwhile, Rafa looked at me stunned. It was somewhat understandable, I had never spoken to her so she had no way of knowing where did I come from.

I admit that, at that moment, I remembered my friend the supermarket cashier who could easily identify me as a foreigner. I felt proud of myself, it seemed that now it wasn't so easy to point me out as foreign guy.

On our way home, I talked with Rafaabout the summer plans. I had two big events in mind, the summer festival organized by the company, and the visit of some friends from Spain. They were going to spend a few days with me in Vorarlberg, more time than enough to visit the best of the area.

6 Summer is the best week of the year

At work things went well, I was gradually integrating into the team and I began to do some things in German. It was the only foreigner among them, so they frequently asked me about the progresses I was making.

Regarding the language, it was still difficult to understand them, not only by my German level but mainly because different dialects were spoken. Each came from a different part of Austria where, as I knew, dialect was different.

Anyway, I had already acquired enough fluency in English so we had no communication problems.

I often asked them about codes of conduct, I was still afraid that cultural differences play a trick on me, but deep inside they were satisfied with having me on the team.

It was due to an email from Corbalán, in which he encouraged me to switch to German, when I decided to take the leap. At first, my decision was taken with great enthusiasm. They found it funny to hear me speak German. But in a few weeks, it went out of control.

Everything was done in German, in dialect actually, and I had to make great efforts to keep up the pace and understand, at least, the most important parts of the conversations. They tried as well to talk in high German, what they did at the beginning, but when someone said something in dialect, all of them switched automatically.

It wasn't long till I gave up requesting them to go back to high German. I was embarrassed to stop meetings every five minutes to ask them to speak more clearly. So almost without realizing it, I was immersed in a jungle of dialects from which I couldn't escape.

The advise of Corbalán was clear: "wait, be patient, don't get overwhelmed and try to enjoy the most". After all, that wasn't different from other situations, the challenge was the same, just the final goal was different.

The fact that it was already summer seemed to help me. Not always weather was nice, in fact here the summer in Vorarlberg was soft, short and unstable, very unstable. At any moment a sunny day could turn into a rainy day. Against all odds, I realized that this instability made me appreciate even more the few days of good weather and try to make the most of them. I was more attentive and motivated than in previous months. Any situation was a great opportunity to improve a bit and understand my teammates a little better.

At that time I was sharing the office with my colleague Marley. He used to receive many phone calls and couldn't help paying attention in order to try guessing whom he was talking to. He was from Tirol, therefore his dialect sounded even stranger to me.

After few months I had learned to differentiate when he was talking with his wife, what happened very often.

I couldn't understand what he said, but I noted that he changed the tone of his voice and answered with an unmistakable "*Hallo Maus*". I learned then that it was the most widespread Austrian loving way to refer to his wife. So, I was curious to know Maus.

In summer the company organized a party at a house near to the mountains. There was food, music and entertainment for the whole family.

I met there Marley, more playful than usual, due in part to the open bar. While I was talking to him, his wife came and I realized that the open bar was also affecting me. Before she introduced herself I recognized her and said,"Oh, I know who you are, hallo Maus!"

And the woman looked at me puzzled, even knowing who I was, she wasn't sure if that level of confidence was typical Spanish or just simple impudence. She looked at her husband looking for an explanation but Marley was immersed watching his almost empty glass, as if he couldn't remember when he had drunk it.

Their children came and then I was definitely sure that the open bar was ruling me. Full of confidence, I tried to speak to them in German. They didn't answered me. They just looked at me with big open eyes. When I stopped talking, they said to his father: "Dad, why your friend speaks so weird?"

But Marley, was still immersed in his research, so I told them: "I come from Spain, there have a dialect a bit weird". The children watched me, pondered, accepted my explanation and ran away searching for new entertainments.

My friend Marley seemed to have completed its investigation and concluded: "Let's go for another drink". We started talking about the plans for summer holidays "So far, I have to prepare something here, two friends are coming this week to spend a few days with me" I said.

Maus joined the conversation and gave me some good ideas. Few days later my friends arrived. We went directly to a terrace, to enjoy the good weather. They didn't expect so much activity on the streets. That was my fault, all winter long I had told them how soon it got dark and how empty the streets were.

Walking around the city, we met a Spanish girl accompanied by an Austrian friend. When I introduced my friends, it came to my mind the difference in the greeting protocols between Spain and Austria. I realized that I haven't told them yet about it. And I didn't, I was curious to see what could happen.

The Austrian girl remained in silence so she went unnoticed till the first brave, after giving two kisses to the Spanish girl, approached her. With catlike reflexes, she dodged the attack and my friend was speechless, without knowing whether he should apologize or ask for explanations.

After that we decided to enjoy the local cuisine, there was a famous castle known by its huge *schnitzels* (coated pork steaks). During the ascent I told them more about the culinary customs of the area, dishes, etc. They couldn't believe so much taste for meat and beer.

I particularly liked the food here, lots of meat, lots of beer, maybe I was missing a bit more of fish but in general I was satisfied.

I told them that it was typical among Spanish newcomers to have any problems during the first year and in Austria, like taking a few extra kilos or as happened to me, going to a medical examination and get a restriction of meat and beer.

They didn't believe me so I had no choice but to tell them what had happened to me. There was a doctor in the area to which all Spaniards were going, mainly because he spoke Spanish. I visit him for routine check. I did some tests and I was summoned next week to discuss the results.

The doctor greeted me in Spanish, with many jokes and a sense of humor that I could hardly understand. It was something I already knew, but I took it as the price to pay for having a doctor who spoke Spanish in Vorarlberg.

"Let's see, Jose, I have here the results of your analysis"here.

"Please, tell me Doctor".

"Look, it's all good in general except the uric acid, is too high".

"I don't know what than means, actually".

"Well, it's not serious, just by changing your diet a little bit, it soon return to healthy levels".

"Okay, no problem, what do I have to change?"

"Well, the fact is that there are three possible reasons that can cause such high levels: excess of meat, seafood or beer'.

And I began to mentally review my diet in the past months, looking for any excess of the mentioned, but nothing, everything seemed normal to me. So I said to the doctor:"Could it be possible Doctor that the analyzes are wrong?"

It wouldn't have been the first time, the doctor was famous in our group because he had confused the names of a Spanish couple who had done the analysis at the same time and gave them the results of each other. Yes, Spanish names are complicated.

"Wrong?, unlikely, why do you think that Jose?".

"Well, I don't remember significant excesses in recent months".

"Well let's see, step by step, tell me, how much meat you eat per week?"

"Up to three days a week, I prefer fish and vegetables".

"Okay, seafood?"

"Almost nothing, maybe once or twice a month".

"Okay, then... beer, do you drink a lot of beer? maybe when going out?"

"Some yes, but not too much".

And the doctor began to review the results of the analysis again, according to my answers it seemed possible that they were wrong. At the same time, my cell phone rang and as I looked for it, I took out my keys and the doctor noticed my unmistakable key chain of Mohren, a local beer brand.

"Jose, you said that you don't drink too much beer".

"Yes, just normal".

"Tell me, how much is normal?".

"You know, 1 or 2 beers a day, nothing more".

"1 or 2 beers daily, is that normal?"

"Of course doctor! Look, 1 = almost nothing, 2 = normal, 3 = average, 4 = party time, 5 = out of control". It was a bad time to try to be funny. The doctor didn't get the joke, completely changed his gesture and shouted at me: "But Jose! that is a liter of beer a day!"

"Well doctor, if you put it that way... of course... it seems like too much...".

But even against the doctor's advice and the beer restriction, we went to the castle. My friends were so confident that those steaks wouldn't be as big as I had told them, that they not only thought they could have one but two. They argued that the hike uphill to the castle would make them hungry enough so to attack the second one.

We sat, ordered and had a coupled of beers while we waited for the food. Few minutes later, two waiters came towards us, carrying huge trays of meat. The face of my friends was a poem, they couldn't believe that.

They looked at the plate, looked at each other uncertainly. We barely managed to finish the first round and didn't even ask if they wanted to try the second round and complete their bet.

After such a feast, we walked a bit through the city. In one of the streets we found a mime doing his show and stopped there for a while to watch him.

We took some photographs but didn't give him any tip. A child approached the mime, gave him a coin and the mime responded with a sequence of precise and elegant movements that casually finished with his finger pointing directly at me.

People standing around was looking at me trying to understand as me, petrified, began to notice the level of the opponent that I had in front of him.

After a moment face to face, both, the mime and me, understood that we were destined to be enemies. There wasn't enough room in the city for both. I realized that in a face to face I could never win, after all he was a professional of standing still. So I had to try something different.

Slowly, I showed him my empty and extended hands as he continued staring straight ahead. Surely he didn't understand what I was doing, but he was aware that, slowly, I was approaching him. Even more slowly, I approached his basket full of coins, with my hands always in his sight. I bent down slightly and I stared at him.

Then he understood what I wanted to do and succumbed to the pressure. He knew that his small fortune was at risk, we were face to face and he wasn't sure of what would be my next move.

My intention was clear, take the basket and run, but it wasn't clear for me if the mime would follow me or not. My move was really good, force a mime to run, there can be anything worse than that. But it was also true that the amount of coins in that basket could justify such dishonor.

Once my hands were really close to the basket, the moment of truth came, I was ready to run. And it was then that the mime looked at me directly, ready to admit the defeat. He blinked twice and I accepted that as a sign of surrender. Accepted his terms, I backed away slowly and the mime blinked again. It was a silent victory, but a victory after all.

The next day I took my friends to the climbing hall, I knew they love it. We had to register and it was there when I became aware of how long my name was for the Austrians. Two names, two surnames, they couldn't understand it since here it's normal to have only one name and one surname.

I tried to explain that to the guy in charge but I failed, I had then to show him my passport, but he didn't still understand why so many names. I think he suspected that it was maybe not even legal.

We spent all day climbing and decide to end up the day with a great dinner. I knew it wasn't a good idea to go to a restaurant without booking a table in advance, so I took it as the perfect opportunity to put into practice my German skills and show to my friends that I was really making progress.

I called one of the restaurants downtown, and the conversation went well until I had to give my name. Here it's important to note that my name uttered by me, heard by Austrian people, can lead to some confusions. My Spanish name sounded to the Austrians as the German word "Hose", trousers.

We went to the restaurant and I told the waitress that we had a reservation.

"Good, name of the reservation please?".

"Jose".

"Ohhh Hose, Mr. Hose."

And the girl quickly called her colleague who was at the bar. They began to talk to each other but I couldn't understand them. Finally the other girl came to us and said in perfect English: "Hello, I am the person whom you spoke earlier by phone".

"Nice to meet you".

"Just a question, should I call Mr. Trousers or Mr. Jeans?" she said as the other girl made huge efforts to not laughing.

"Excuse me?"

"Yes, I have here your reservation, Mr. Hose. We appreciate the sense of humor, so tell me, Mr. Trousers or Mr. Jeans?"

My friends understood the joke even not knowing German and joined the girls laughing. Everyone was having a great time because of Mr. Hose, except me.

The next day my friends had to return to Spain, they liked so much the area and were happy to see that I had finally found a place where I was happy. We spent the morning remembering old times, the time we worked together, those conversations about the future, where we would like to work, as we imagined it would be, etc.

One of them told me that I should be proud of what I was achieved, something that surprised me.

He had been always a reference for me, it was much better programmer than I was and he had that emotional intelligence which it made so easy to work with him, even when he had reasons to be angry, he talked to me in a way that I didn't feel bad, all the contrary, I just wanted to go back immediately to work to fix my mistakes.

And there he was, telling me that "it was a pleasure to see how I got what I always wanted to have". He smiled and said: "you probably don't remember, but many years ago, but we had already talked about this place".

I didn't know what he was talking about. He took his phone and showed me a video of a party, many, many years ago. We were there, talking, surrounded by beers and food, while I was explaining how it would be, for me, the ideal company to work for.

I wasn't only describing the company I was currently working for in Vorarlberg but also the area.

I began to remember and my friend was right, at that time we complained about the inhuman amount of hours we worked and that we had no time even to do some sport and relax.

He also reminded me that I often said: "would it be easier to live in peace, go down the street and say hello to everyone? at the end the most important is to have fun, right?".

It was undoubtedly the best gift he could ever gave to me. Now I was aware of how lucky I was to be where I was. If it were not for him, I probably never would have realized that, what I had in Austria was what I always wanted to have.

I thought a lot about that during the following days, I vividly recalled those conversations and the more I thought about it, the more certain I was that it couldn't just be a coincidence.

I wrote to Corbalán and told him about that. His answer was basically the same that he gave me the day we met at the airport. I shared that opinion, but maybe after so many battles and struggles, I had decided to forget it for a while to focus on the daily problems.

It was the moment to reflect on my current situation, so I did that during the weekend. I was acceptably happy but I couldn't help to wonder if it could be even better, and if that was the case, what could I do to improve my life.

I told myself: "Step by step. Let's start by improving the relationship with Barnie, I like him, and partly thanks to him I have achieved a lot so far". I contacted again Corbalán, convinced that my new approach was right and he would approve it. His answer marked my way of seeing things in coming months. Full of metaphors, his answer said:

"If you squeeze an orange, orange juice will come up. But if you squeeze an apple, you can't expect orange juice to come out. Life, people, continually puts pressure on us, and is what we have inside, what comes out. If you react with negative emotions, it's because you had them already inside you, and that's no one fault's but yours, it's entirely your responsibility. Fill yourself with positive thoughts and you will see that it doesn't matter what happens to you, only positive emotions will come out".

As I would say in Spanish: "immense Corbalán, immense". He left me speechless.

So I committed to follow his advice. His words resounded constantly in my head and I started looking at every situation from a new point of view, analyzing and scrutinizing every thought that crossed my mind, embracing the positive ones and discarding the negative ones.

My relationship with Barnie change dramatically in a matter of days, now I saw him as a nice caring guy, not as someone full of insecurities and complexes that had built a shield to protect from the rest of the people.

"My best friend of Bludenz", I began to call him. It was true that he was the only one I knew from that city but he didn't care. The title of best friend filled him with joy and joined the game.

With his particular sense of humor, he came one day to my office claiming I was his best friend from Spain. During the day he took each opportunity to cry out to the four winds that I was his best friend from Spain.

To celebrate such a special friendship, Barnie offered me a complete plan: movies and table football with his friends. How could I reject that. We went to the movies to watch a science fiction movie, a genre that both liked. The movie was, of course, in German.

It was the first time I went to the movies in Austria and the first big surprise was that the people didn't go to the movies with popcorn but with the full dinner, nachos, beer, whatever they liked.

I can't say I understood the entire film, but enough to follow the plot. It was about parallel universes, from a very realistic point of view. We left the cinema discussing the possibilities of that being real and if so, how it would be a parallel universe, what differences respect our it would have.

Barnie explained excited that perhaps in a parallel universe, he was moving to Spain and we knew there, we worked together and we became also best friends.

We arrived at the place where his friends were waiting for us, willing to play table football. Introductions made, we started playing after ordering the necessary beers.

The table football that I was used to in Spain was the one in which players have two legs, a 3-3-4 formation and the goals higher than the center, which caused such an inclination that the ball always fell towards the center of the table.

But in Austria it was different, they have the international model, in which players have only one leg and a different formation. Still with the topic of the movie in my mind, I found myself thinking "hey look, I am in the parallel universe".

But we started playing and I got a little scared. I was expecting the ball to fall down the center of the table but it didn't, it went up. When I expected the ball to move, It stopped. The laws of physics as I knew them have completely changed.

Maybe I was actually in the parallel universe. However, there was one thing that remained the same, the ball went from one side to another and I wasn't able to react in time.

In those days, Barnie was on cloud nine, we got together to watch a Spanish football match and he was so happy there, surrounded by Spaniards, talking to them in Spanish, just having fun.

After the game we went out with the bad luck that I met my landlord down the street. I greeted him and he told me he was about to call me. Now he wanted an even bigger deposit and in a bank account, not in cash. He urged me to go to the bank as soon as possible and make the necessary arrangements.

I didn't have the courage to discuss with him about that so I accepted the mission and next Monday I went to the bank to make the new deposit.

I still remembered my last visit to the bank, months ago, and tried to convince that Lady Bank will not be there, maybe she was already retired, or in holidays. But deep, deep down I knew she would be there, waiting for me, with the best of her smiles.

And indeed, my dear Lady Bank was there, early in the morning, still sleepily. As soon as I entered the bank she instantly recognized me and woke up, as a child to the smell of freshly baked cake. That I was for her, the sweet of the day.

But this time I remembered the three fundamental laws that I had learned in the past, I thought I was better prepared.

First law:Lady Bank doesn't appreciate punctuality.

I arrived at the bank few minutes after opening, Lady Bank had already finished her breakfast. First test passed.

Second law:Lady Bank is always right.

After a while explaining what I wanted to do, in the best way I could, Lady Bank agreed to proceed:

"Well, now go to the cash dispenser and get the money".

"But the cashier is not going to make so much money, it will exceed the limit".

"Just do it, please".

"Ok, I go".

And as expected, the cash dispenser refused to give me so much money. I went back to Lady Bank, begging for mercy: "It says that it's too much money".

"Normal, that's the wrong cash dispenser. You have to go to that counter, give me your credit card, and I will give you the money". Definitely she was playing with me and she liked it.

Third law: Lady Bank never gets tired.

And with my small fortune in his hands, the mood of Lady Bank changed, she was just abou to smile. She explained to me in German the following steps but I couldn't follow her, I was exhausted. Aware of her superiority, she decided to end the game and told me: "sign here and here and you're done".

7 | Born to rule the mountains

The summer was short but intense but almost without noticing it, winter, feared and loved at the same time, was about to come. Within a few weeks, good temperatures disappeared, days shortened quickly and the people was talking more about ski than barbecues.

In my team there was some expectation about me and the winter. This was the year that was supposed to learn to ski. From scratch, in an area where children learn to ski almost before they can walk. It wasn't my first winter in Vorarlberg, but the first I would have to face the mountains.

In the previous year I had postponed the skiing just to focus my efforts in getting used to everything else, I had more than enough in my plate.

For me, the arrival of winter was marked for lack of daylight. Go to work before dawn, go home when it was already dark. It took me some days to get used to that. Anyway I was still fascinated to see from the valley all the snowy mountains, it was a privilege to have these views from home and from the office.

It was also a constant reminder that this winter, without excuses, I must learn to ski, face my fears and master the snow.

Barnie didn't let pass the occasion to remind me how quickly the opening of the season was approaching. I had already all prepared and had decided to go with the Spanish group. Indeed, there were in that group more beginners like me so I thought that perhaps learning with them would be more bearable.

The first days were terrible, lots of falls, exhaustion and tiny progress, much less than I expected. The problem itself wasn't falling or learning. The problem was to deal with the so-called experts all day long. How easy must it be for someone who has ski all his life: "just put the body weight forward and you're done, it's easy". Sure. Not easy, very easy.

Barnie took that to the next level, he cheered me up, filmed videos of me, but I still liked him. After some days, I had fell down so many times I was able to fake falls without being noticed it was on purpose.

When Barnie was especially tiresome, I just wait for some girl passing next to me, fake a fall and wait there till she came to help me. All stopped to ask me if I was ok. I talked to all of them. And Barnie watched me, puzzled.

The other difficult part of digest were children. It was so easy for them to learn. Just in a matter of hours. Totally demoralizing. Still, I kept trying and trying despite multiple falls.

One day, skiing with the Spanish group, I stopped counting the falls when I reached hundred. I was very tired and in the last attempt I made the mistake of trying to save the fall and felt a little hamstring strain.

I understood that as a sign to go home. But in the group didn't see it that way, they wanted to hasten the last hours of the day. After several minor discussions, they convinced me to return to the lift with them. "On the top, at the end of the ift, there is a bar, you can wait for us there while having a drink. Then we all leave together" they said.

It didn't sound so bad, I like the bars of ski resorts, good views, hot coffee in the middle of the mountains. Nice.

So I accepted the offer and got in the lift with them. When we were reaching the top I began to suspect that something was wrong. My friends were too silent, some smiled devilish. But nobody told me anything. We go there and I forgot about the bar, I was just focused on getting off the lift without falling down again.

I barely did it and when I stopped, I looked up searching for that oasis in the middle the snow, the promised bar. But it wasn't there. In front of me, forest. On the left a red track and Spanish group often looking like a monkey in a zoo. On the right a black track and another group of Spanish making efforts to not laugh. No, I couldn't believe it, there was no bar.

After a few moments of laughter, accusations and vows, I accepted the reality, I had to make a choice: red or black. Or going down on the lift. But my friends opposed to that option, what a dishonor. It was too much pressure. So I chose the red track. Tired and with muscle problems I did my best and got down slowly but safe.

During the following weeks we went back to skiing as much as possible. We were not experts yet but small progress could be seen every weekend. The holiday season was approaching and the first part of the ski season was about to finish. I couldn't wait to go back to Spain and see my family again, one year after. I wanted to tell them all my news, how good it was and how happy I was. But before we had the Christmas party of the company.

Similar to other parties but with the difference that it took place in the same building we worked and all employees were coming. And there was open bar. The risk was huge.

During the party, I was with Rafa and other Spanish employees having some drinks. We were talking about trivial issues when we saw that the CEO of the company was walking towards us.

He began to ask us about the integration, the people, the language, etc. Although he was kind man, he was still the CEO and we the newcomers so nobody dared to complain too much.

But Rafa was made of sterner stuff. Tanning in a thousand battles, he knew no fear. And he started complaining about what it most could hurt someone from here, his dialect.

"Well, with the language still not so good" told Rafa to the CEO.

"But you already speak quite good" said the CEO.

"Yes but I still have problems with the dialect. There are people who literally I don't understand anything they say".

And as the CEO tried to be more understanding, Rafa kept going until the CEO said: "Look, we can do this if you want, I will help you with the dialect, I will give you lessons".

And Rafa wasn't expecting that, he didn't know what to answer and was speechless. I tried to help him "Rafa, come on, it's the opportunity you were looking for, you will learn dialect!"

Never before had Rafa looked at me with so much hate. Then the CEO decided to chase me as well: "Well, I can also teach you".

"That's it, teach him, teach him" exclaimed Rafa.

"Thank you but I have more than enough for the moment with my tandems" I replied.

After the CEO left, Rafa and me continued enjoying the party. We felt that the worst part was over, now it was time to have some fun. And there was open bar.

One might think that the biggest difference between Austria and Spain are the drinks, we like more the cocktails and the shots, they like more the beer. In part that's true, but here they aren't limited to beer, drinking here is a real thing. If the beer runs out, people keep toasting with wine or whatever is at hand.

In addition to beer, I found somethings quite new to me. I remember that during my first week I was invited to a Christmas market in which the star drink was the sweet warm wine. What a discovery.

We went to the open bar looking for something new. There were cards with available cocktails, all known, margaritas, daiquiris, caipirinhas. Rafa stepped forward to order and asked me:

"What do you want Jose?"

"Caipirinha".

"Caipirina? caipirinha is for girls".

"Ok, what you going to drink?"

"Caipiroska my way".

"Caipiroska your way?"

"Yes, do you know what it is?"

"I don't know, caipirinha but with vodka instead of rum?"

"That would be still for girls".

"Please, enlighten me Rafa...".

"Caipiroska my way: from the caipirinha keep only the rum, the rest fill it with vodka".

The party continued and the open bar as well. The next thing I remember was taking a taxi with some Austrians to continue the party in an apartment. Against all odds, partying here was much better than I expected. On that apartment there were many people, two large groups, one formed for Spaniards, the other for Austrian people.

Encouraged by alcohol, a couple of brave guys had a brilliant idea: "we could take advantage of the good atmosphere, the Spaniards will speak in German and the Austrians will speak in Spanish".

To which an Austrian replied "Good idea, in that way tomorrow we won't have bad conscience for the hangover, we will have at least practiced languages".

On paper the idea wasn't bad, the problem was that no one decided to start. In the end, we are all shy, but of course, everything changes when alcohol is involved. After the second round of drinks, some sentences in German with Spanish accent were heard.

One more round and some Austrian dared with Spanish. In the fifth round, English couldn't be heard anymore, Spaniards were talking in German and Austrians in Spanish. The idea was a complete success.

I saw as Rafa was drinking at a higher rate than usual. He looked more and more comfortable speaking German as he kept drinking. Soon he began to feel sick and decide to go out to the terrace to get some fresh air. Good idea.

A few minutes later he entered back quickly shouting: "Quick, I need pen and paper!, go go!"

"Pencil and pa... come on Rafa, take another beer..." I replied.

"No, no, I need something to write, come on" he said. I didn't understand what he was doing, butRafa continued:"come on, from the terrace you can see the mountains, and there is someone there trying to communicate with me!"

I didn't know what to answer to that, he looked so convinced that I just believed him. I went to the terrace with him, to see what kind of entity wanted to communicate with Rafa. And indeed, there was something there.

While Rafa wrote down dots and dashes like crazy, I just realized that cars were driving down the mountain, which added to the trees of the forest, had made Rafa to believe that someone was talking to him in Morse code.

I could tell him but he looked so excited. It was the perfect night for him, he had had a good time, learned some German, and now he was deciphering hidden messages. I left him there, complaining that the message didn't make any sense and I returned to the party.

Even the deplorable conditions I found myself the next day, I had to put myself together. It was the day that I was flying back to Spain for Christmas, two weeks of well-deserved vacation.

I had left everything prepared the day before, even the coffee. So my biggest challenge was to wake up and get to the station on time. I knew I could do it, come on, lets go. Next stop Munich.

It was the first time I was traveling from Munich. I arrived at the station just in time. Among the rush and stress, I got as I could to the platform to catch the train to the airport.

I heard something on the loudspeaker, in German, something like people going to the airport should sit towards the back of the train, but I didn't give it much importance.

I got in the train, sat, and started reviewing the train tickets, boarding pass, passport, etc. I raised my head and saw that in front of me there were a lady sleeping and beside her, a small child staring at me.

"What's up big man?" I told him.

"You shouldn't be here" he replied.

"What do you say?"

"This is not your place".

"Ahm, where is it my place then?" asked a bit scared.

"You must go to the other side"

"The other side?"

"If not, you'll never catch your flight".

"But what are you saying kid?"

"Very soon, the train will split in half... and you will loose your flight...".

I was really frightening. His mother woke up, and after seeing my face told the boy: "What have I told you about bothering people, eh?, what have I told you?".

"Nothing, ignore him please, he just gets bored in the train" said the lady to me. She saw that I had the boarding pass on my hands and said: "If you go to the airport, you should go to the other side of the train".

"Why is that?"

"At the next stop, the train splits into two trains, one is going to the airport and the other goes back".

o after some more hours of traveling, I finally came to Spain, to my house. And immediately I realized how much I missed the people and the food. I found it interesting that only when I was in Spain was really aware of how lucky I was to be in Vorarlberg. In every conversation, I could find points of contrast which, till then I hadn't noticed.

When talking to my friends, most of them working in Spain, I realized how good my job was. The topics of the conversations, which hadn't changed in years, were most about complaints about bosses, lack of opportunities, etc. An atmosphere of resignation, in which I had participated also in the past, without even aware of it.

When talking to the few of them who were abroad, the conversations were very different. We all shared something, we were proud of the decision that one day we had made and if we would have to make it again, we would without hesitation.

I tried to spend as much time as possible with my family, especially my parents. The interrogation seemed endless but it didn't bother me. From the food to the weather, everything seemed interesting to them. At first.

After the first week, my mother had already gathered enough information and related all of them to northern Spain, concluding that the differences were minimal.

And she was right, except for the snow, both regions were quite similar. And that was something that certainly had played in my favor, it had made it easier for me, to adapt to the new environment.

Often my mother was asked about what she thought that I would have gone so far, nothing more and nothing less than 1000 kilometers from home. To which, she always replied with the same tranquility,"200, 500, 1000, it's all the same. If he has to come here to something, it will take him the same amount of time. And Skype works equally well at 200, 500 or 1000 kilometers. Moreover, I prefer he is far and happy, that closer but unhappy. It's not worth".

Those two weeks in Spain helped me to realize what I had in Austria, what I had achieved. After so many months in a row there, I took many things as granted. It was normal not to stress at work, it was normal to leave office soon, it was normal to have free time. It was normal to enjoy life every day.

But once back in Spain, although I knew it was for a short time, I put everything in contrast, past memories, conversations with friends.

Everything reminded me of the differences between what I had now and what I had before.

That was a very good feeling. And unexpected. I was really motivated, thinking about what I could achieve next year once again in Austria. It was the first time that I was really excited about my Christmas tradition of setting personal goals for the next year.

With so much emotion inside me, I wanted to share that and although people are happy for me, I doubt they would see it the same way. The only one who could fully understand me was Corbalán, so I sent him an email describing my feelings of those days in Spain. He responded enthusiastically and happy for me:

"I'm glad that everything goes well. Spend as much time as you can with your family because time flies so fast. It will be a while until you come back again, they will miss you so focus on them. You will have your reward when you come back to Austria. I will not advance anything else, you will discover it by yourself soon".

It was common in his answers hiding something that I couldn't imagine. I didn't know what he could mean this time. I didn't think there was anything else of Austria that I didn't know so far and could still surprise me.

Holidays were finished and I returned to Vorarlberg. Next day I started working again. Since the alarm went off I was already envisioning what Corbalán meant in its response.

The contrast, again. Now I was back to my routine with renewed strengths and a new point of view. The days in Spain had refreshed my memory and now I could appreciate the differences and I was filled with a sense of gratitude throughout the day.

There was no need to tell Corbalán, he already knew that would occur to me, as it probably happened to him in the past. Another curious thing was that after two weeks without practicing any German, I hadn't forgotten almost nothing, I even found it easier to talk during those days.

As I discovered later, there were two reasons for that. Holidays in Spain had served me to disconnect. At the same time, all that I had studied and practiced have had time enough to settle down in my memory and be available when needed, once back in Austria.

8 Moving on

After a few days, I began to understand what they meant the rest of Spaniards when they spoke of post-holiday syndrome. Until then, it seemed to me like an exaggeration, one more reason to complain, but unreal.

But this time I was wrong, they were right. Two weeks in Spain and I was used to relax, food, family. Going back was hard. The first few weeks were hard.

Our main occupation during the weekend was skiing. I was already the king of the falls, breaking records every weekend but at least, I saw some progress which kept me motivated.

Barnie, expert skier, constantly invited me to go with him but I politely rejected the offer because I didn't think I was ready yet. I was still going with the Spanish group. Which was perfect for me, it is always fine to find people with the same problems that you. There were also experts who occasionally gave good advices, which I also appreciated.

I discovered another great difference of working in Vorarlberg. Most of my colleagues, also skiers, selected carefully the days to go skiing. Preferably sunny but cold days, it didn't happen ofter but those were the perfect conditions for skiing early in the morning.

Those days it was common for many to not work and go to the nearest station, or skiing in the morning and working in the afternoon.

This would be unthinkable in Spain and I was eager to try it. It seemed an incredible breakthrough in terms of reconciling work and personal life.

I mentioned it to Rafa, also expert skier, and since we worked in the same company and the idea seemed interesting to him, we started to go skiing together on weekdays. Obviously, he was way faster than me, but it was a situation good for both of us.

He didn't care of going down alone and it was a constant challenge for me trying to follow him. He forced me to improve and there was no pressure.

In addition, we got along pretty well, Rafa was very clear when speaking his mind, didn't use mince words, always open-minded. That distinguished him from the critical section of the Spanish group, so prone to complain for no apparent reason and criticize everything they didn't like it.

When I was more confident in the snow, he began to challenge me in order to make me improve more, for example, trying the toughest tracks in the station. I remember nostalgically the first time I faced a black track. My dear black track. It began with the largest slope that can be experienced in this part of Austria, Diaboloabfahrt in Golm. What an experience.

At that point I was no longer worried about falling, in that I was already an expert. But the track was so steep that my body had decided to ignore my orders. I found myself trying to turn and my legs telling me no, under these conditions they wouldn't move.

A few more failed attempts and at the third try I went down doing turns instead of just letting me slide. It was certainly an achievement, not only because I hadn't fallen but because I was still in one piece.

The next challenge was a bit more complicated. The track had an uphill half way, so according to the explanations of Rafa, I had to face it at high speed to crown it.

Otherwise, I should walk and given its slope could be almost impossible. The added difficulty was that the approaching to that uphill was done in a curve. At that time, I didn't give it the importance that it really had.

Rafa had drawn up a plan which he said would make things easier for me. He would go down first and wait for me at the top of the hill. From there, he could see me and tell me when I should start to speed up.

I began my descent and before reaching the hill, I ran down the curve faster than I was able to handle. I tried to turn to slow down when I realized that Rafa was yelling at me, I wasn't fast enough for him. I tried to made the curve and speed up at the same time. That was the challenge.

I knew I couldn't make it, but the idea of walking uphill didn't excite me so I kept going and try my best. As expected, when the speed increased, I lost control of the curve and fell precipitously. Fortunately I was fine, but the fall was very long, about 20-25 meters. I was standing in the middle of the track, far away from where the fall began. I couldn't even see where my sticks had landed.

Crowning the hill, there he was, Rafa laughing out loud. I wait there for more people to come down and help me get to pick up my things. I walked toward the slope. Rafa was still there, doing his best to survive that attack of laughter.

Even after that, we came back many times. We used to start very early in the morning, when the snow was perfect, and leave soon, when we had skied enough and the tracks began to be full of people.

In the Spanish group that was unthinkable, they preferred to start later, take it easy and stay there till the station was closing.

I was still going with them from time to time because it was funny skiing in a large group, to rest, to have lunch together, etc. I failed to convince Rafa to join the group, he preferred going alone. He knew Barnie, I proposed to invite him to ski with us but he was neither thrilled by the idea.

Barnie kept going with his invitation. I began to suspect that so many rejections from me, could be taken the wrong way from him, so I proposed him to join the Spanish group.

At first he didn't seem that as a very good idea but I managed to convince him that it was a great opportunity to improve his Spanish, meet girls. I said to him "well, you're going to be the best skier of the group, everybody will admire you". That was enough to change his mind.

A couple of weeks later, Barnie joined us. it wasn't the best day for skiing because the visibility was very poor. It was my first time in those conditions and it was a very strange feeling, not knowing, literally, what would you find in the following meters.

People didn't like to ski in those conditions so we decided to spend the afternoon in one of the restaurants of the station. And there, Barnie, after a couple of beers was the man.

It took him very few time to get along with other Spaniards thanks to his unique charisma. He was encouraged to say something in Spanish, the ones who could speak German dared to ask him about the dialect, etc. He was enjoying so much attention.

After having lunch and some beers, Barnie led a group that went away to play hammering, something typical here. The one who hammers a nail before the others is the winner. Simple.

But soon the started with the shots. And then Barnie came to me, singing something in German and proclaiming to the four winds that I was his best friend from Spain and he could never ever imagine that he would have such a good time.

Occasionally he returned skiing with us, he did what he could to reconcile that new group with his lifelong friends. His great interest was to join us in spring or summer, since he knew the stories about the barbecues and was something that he definitely wanted to try.

Meanwhile, I continued talking with some friends in Spain to plan a visit to Austria. It wasn't easy to agree and the only dates found, coincided with the birthday of a friend who was living in Germany.

We talked with him, and he invited us to his birthday party, there, in Germany. For me it was especially interesting to know the group of Spaniards who lived with him in Germany. I wanted to see the differences with my group here.

As expected, it was a group of friendly people, but to my surprise they didn't speak German better than us.

I was convinced that living in an area without dialect would make it easier to learn German but it wasn't the case. As it happened to us, the fact that people speak English was also an obstacle for them, they were not forced to speak in German.

One thing was different, there were almost no complaints about the country or the people. Most of the conversations were about the possibilities of going back to Spain. Fewer complaints and more homesickness, I would define it that way.

And I was curious about that because salaries were higher there. It seemed to me that they preferred going back to Spain regardless the work conditions. That gave me an idea of how much they missed their country. Which also meant that maybe they were not especially successful with the integration.

It's true that my group complained a lot, but the option of returning to Spain was always out of the table. I think that the reason for that was that we were minimally integrated in Vorarlberg, ones more than others.

We spent the weekend there with our friend and his German girlfriend, who spoke some Spanish, and I couldn't miss the opportunity I make a joke on my friend.

The first thing his girlfriend told me, in a very decent Spanish, was to give her all advices that I had about the language, to what I replied: "whenever he ask you anything, you just answer: you'd better know". It took her less than five minutes to put it into practice.

"Honey, should we go shopping now?" told my friend to his girlfriend.

"You'd better know".

And my friend was puzzled.

"Do you want to call your friend?".

"You'd better know".

We were driving and my friend looked at me slyly looking for some clue. We went to buy some things for the party and when we were a bit away from her, he told me "she's angry with me, but I have no idea why".

"Do you really think so?"

"Yes, she seems very pissed off, I must done something...".

"No, I don't think so".

And I told her:"Do you know where the pizzas are?"

"Yes, in that direction".

And my friend said to her: "what about the ice?"

"You'd better know".

I ended confessing during the party and my friend, a bit angry at the beginning, took it well finally.

We continue with the party and I got a call from my landlord, something was wrong again with the deposit but I couldn't understand very well, mainly because of his dialect.

What better opportunity to show to that group, how real problems with a dialect looked like. I put my landlord on the speaker I could see on their faces that they didn't understand anything.

After long explanations, I came to the conclusion that what he meant was that I had to change the account where I had the deposit. He had delegated the management of his apartments to an agency and now they were in charge of the deposits as well. My mission that time was to take the money out of the account and give it to the agency. Again, I had to face Lady Bank.

We continued the party and next morning we said goodbye to my friend. During the trip back to Vorarlberg I kept thinking about my last encounter with Lady Bank. I went to the bank next Monday and there she was, my dear lady, just waiting for me, the sweet of the day. That time I just ignored her three fundamental laws, I felt really confident.

"Hello, I wanted to take all the money out of this account".

"But this account is not only at your name" she told me.

"I know, is for the apartment where I live, the landlord and me share this account".

He asked for my ID, information about the flat. It seemed that, after our history, she didn't still trust me so much.

"What is the password?".

"The password of what?"

"Of the account, what it's the account password?"

I had no idea that such an account might have a password. Or maybe the landlord had told me at some point and I didn't get it.

I told Lady Bank I didn't know the password and she started to worry till she said: "So you want to get all the money from an account that is not only at your name, and you don't know the password".

It sounded very bad but I answered quite naturally.

"That's it".

The lady continued to review my documents, checked my passport again and said "and you're Spanish" which it seemed not generating much confidence to her.

"Well, without the password I can't give you anything".

That definitely didn't look good. "Yes, but look, it's the account for the deposit, it's actually my money" I told her.

And in a goodwill gesture, Lady Bank looked at me and said: "Then the password is...?".

I looked doubtfully few seconds, that seemed unreal to me. Finally I said: "deposit?"

"Okay, that is. Now I can give you the money".

I got out of there as fast as I could, with the money, fearing that Lady Bank decided to rectify and put me even more problems.

My friends meanwhile had spent the day skiing in the area, taking advantage of the last day before returning to Spain.

I joined them the next day and I thanked the lessons from Rafa.

Thanks to him I could follow them, they had more experience than me but apparently the tracks in Spain were generally easier than in Austria.

In the following weeks, I tried to go skiing as much as I could, especially on weekends. But the closer the end of the season was, the more I struggled to get up early in the morning to go to the station.

The weather began to improve, spring was just around the corner. We looked forward to the arrival of the sun. Winter, cold and full of snow, wasn't particularly hard. Here it helped the geography of the area, located in a valley that protected it from strong winds.

This was a regular conversation with my family, they took for granted that here the cold was unbearable but nothing further from reality. No doubt I had been colder in the past in other cities in Spain than here.

It's true that without so much snow, very little, but with lower temperatures and winds that made literally impossible to go out some days.

This year I was determined to make the most of the sunny days. Among my goals were, relative to sports, biking and hiking. The nature in Vorarlberg was a privilege, with plenty of routes and places to go hiking or cycling. It was the time then, to explore the area.

Moreover, as it happened with skiing, I had also plenty of support for that. There was a Spanish subgroup that love biking and almost everyone enjoyed hiking. There was also Barnie, an expert in both subjects.

The first day that seemed good for biking, I picked up my bike very early in the morning and attacked a fairly famous route in the area, which ended at the top of a mountain where there was a restaurant and a viewpoint.

It wasn't long, just five kilometers, but steep. I suffered a lot, but after some stops I came up to the top in about an hour. The effort certainly deserved it because the views were spectacular, one could see the entire valley from the viewpoint.

I made a break up and decided to go to the restaurant to drink, I felt I deserved it. But when I looked for my wallet, my worst fears were realized, I had lost it, with all the cards inside.

Also money, 30 euros, but I didn't care about that. In the past, whenever I heard that someone had lost his wallet or purse, I couldn't help thinking how hard and boring it would be to recover all of them again.

I went down scanning inch by inch the floor but I wasn't able to find it. I got home thinking about where I could have possibly lost it. I had only made three stops, only one to eat something.

Something that I had in the same pocket of the wallet. Maybe I was so tired that it had fallen without me noticed it. Yes, it should be there. I had come back to recover it.

As I was preparing to my return, someone rang the doorbell but I decided not to open. He insisted again and saw out the window as a car was leaving, it seemed that no one would bother me anymore. The truth is that I wasn't in the mood to talk to anyone at that time, even less in German. I was focused just in finding my wallet.

I went back to the mountain and repeated the way. I got again to the top without success. I went down again, looking around but no signs of the wallet. I arrived home defeated and powerless. Just wanting to lay on the bed.

While I was there, laying and feeling sorry for the time I would lose recovering all I had inside the wallet, a came a question raised in my mind. Who would knock on my door so early in the morning, a weekday?.

It could be the postman, but the mailboxes were out, maybe I had a package, no it couldn't be, they always were delivered to the company.

And I came to the conclusion that, perhaps someone had found the wallet and had just brought to me. In Spain it would be improbable but here it could be.

In that was case, since I didn't open the door, the logical next step would be to left it in the mailbox. Suddenly my strength came back and run to the mailbox. I opened it and the wallet was there, with everything inside, even the money.

The euphoria of the moment disappeared when I realized that I would never be able to thank the person who bothered to bring my wallet back and even had the decency to not keeping the money that it was inside.

9 | Spanish hero

With the arrival of the summer holidays, dozens of interns joined the company, excited to work and be part of such an international environment.

To my surprise, among them was the Austrian girl, the girl of the train, she had joined to the cleaning crew. She told me that it wasn't a job she liked but she must do it since she needed the money to go to college next year.

In our team it was a tradition that the interns brought a cake before finishing their practices. That year, we welcomed two very friendly interns and decided to update the tradition so we told tell them that they should bring two cakes, one to celebrate his arrival to the team, one to celebrate they were leaving. Just a goodwill gesture from them.

They gladly accepted the new tradition and agreed to fulfill it before the end of their first week. They quickly integrated into the team, they contributed to create a a very good atmosphere. The jokes were common because both had the same name, which usually led to misunderstandings.

At the end of the week they came to the office, one bringing a cake, the other bringing beers. The explanation was simple, why bringing two cakes when they could bring cake and beer?. Everyone was fine with that. After some beers, a proposal came up to end confusing them once and for all.

Barnie, sharp as always, was thinking about the issue while tasting the cake and finishing his beer:"a great apricot cake indeed, I will call you... MCake. A great beer, I will call you... NoCake". Now officially, the interns were already part of the team.

I often met the Austrian girl in the company. Always smiling, she stopped for a while and we talked about everything. Step by step, we got closer, we were getting along pretty well.

One day she was upset, a mystery, apparently someone was throwing rests of fruit not in the trash but in the drawers of silverware. Strange. Without more information it was impossible to find out who was the guilty one, so I recommended her to pay attention, any detail could be a crucial clue. Two days later he came up with a possible suspect.

"Whenever I clean and I find that, I see a guy leaving the coffee corner, it has to be him".

"But you can't prove it".

"No".

"And you can't catch him in the act".

"No, because he heard me coming. I'm telling you, it must be him, I know it.".

"Ok, calm down, look, if you can't prove that he is guilty, check if he behaves like an innocent one".

"How?"

"Face him. Yell at him. Petite angry girls are scary, believe me".

And so she did. The next day she found that guy in the coffee corner, she gave him a talk about how easy it was to throw the trash in its place but the guy didn't care and replied: "I don't know what you're talking about, I'm just an intern, I just do the work that others don't want to do".

At first I thought it was just a joke, but this was something else. That guy wasn't an intern, I knew he had been working in the warehouse for several years.

I suspected that was perhaps he was frustrated. After so many years working there, interns came and could do the same as him, maybe even better without much effort.

So, arrogant and overbearing. I told Corbalán and even though I was sure that guy deserved a lesson, Corbalán recommended caution: "you're not 100% sure that it was him. At least not yet. When you are sure, then yes, he will be an enemy and as such, must be defeated. But if you're wrong, he will suffer your anger without deserving it, you will be then the enemy and therefore, you will deserve to be defeated".

Wise words. I was thinking about it for several days until I had the chance to test that guy. In the morning I was having a coffee with the girl and the guy passed by. He couldn't help to smile shyly. Now I knew it was him.

I went for lunch with Barnie and I sat behind the guy, back to back, one meter of distance was separating us. My first instinct was to get up, throw my dishes him and crown revenge by saying: "oh my God, what a mess, well, at least we both would agree that it's better to throw trash in its place, right?"

But that was precisely what Corbalán invited me to avoid. So I decide to do something more subtle, at the end my goal was just helping the girl.

I told Barnie:"Pay attention to what I'm going to do, I may need in the future a confirmation of it to third parties". And Barnie watched me very closely.

When I stood up, I hit the guy with my chair. No rush to apologize, I gave him time enough to turn around and to see that it was me. I was expecting that he would think: "the same guy who was in the morning with the girl, that can't be a coincidence".

And immediately I sent a message to the girl: "my plan is set, there are 25% of probabilities that you never find again the trash out of place".

And I explained everything to Barnie, including the 25%:

"The guy may be smart or not, coward or not. There is a 25% of chances that he's smart and coward at the same time. If he's smart, he would know who I am and that I've hit him on purpose. He saw me talking with the girl, so he would deduce that she told me about the trash. And if he's coward, he will stop it, what kind of coward would want to get into trouble with a stranger. Moreover, if he investigate on me and finds out I'm not from here, that I have nothing to lose, the only possible smart move is to don't do it anymore".

Some weeks passed and the girl didn't have anymore problems with that guy.

After the success of my first act as a superhero, the Austrian girl was delighted and felt safer, so much that she told me another problem she had. She wasn't expecting me to do anything about it, we just had confidence enough so she could tell me about this kind of things.

She said that in those summer months, despite the intermittent heat, she preferred to come to work as stuffy as possible because there were people who were always staring at women. And that was a situation she wanted to avoid, it made her feel very uncomfortable.

I asked more about that and found that there was in the company an old man, about 50 years, constantly staring at her, without any respect, even outlining some smile as she found really irritating.

That man didn't care about that she was feeling uncomfortable, he even tried sometimes to talk to her and although she responded angrily, he continued behaving in the same way.

I knew that man, I had already seen him doing that. Since the conversation with the Austrian girl I watched him closely and it was clear for me that behind that facade of arrogance there were no more than weaknesses and complexes. Even for his age, he seemed to be in good shape. However, he was usually dressing more like a teenager than a man close to retirement.

I didn't have any specific plan to help the Austrian girl with that, but it was clear for me that I would take any change I would have to do something about it.

I text Corbalán and he responded briefly but eloquently as always:

"the universe provides the opportunity to those who seek and deserve them".

It wasn't the first time he had told me me about that. I still remember the first discussion we had about definitions, in which we argued about terms like fate, destiny. According to him, all of them invented for us in the past to define something that we were not able to fully understand.

Corbalánthought that there were simply mechanisms of the universe, that we had named in order to understand them, but at the end they didn't exist as such. Just an universe, working according to its rules, rules still unknown for most of us.

That time I decided to not question his words, I simply accepted that fate or the universe or whatever would provide an opportunity to help my Austrian girl as I thought it would be fair.

Next time that I talked to her, I promised he to solve the problem, I didn't know how or when, but I asked her to trust me, just as I was trusting the words of Corbalán.

After some days, the girl wrote me one day to take a break in the afternoon. I had a meeting that afternoon so we agreed to see us when I were finished.

The meeting itself was an open discussion on the status of the project, necessary because we were nearing at the end and there was a considerable delay.

The causes for the delay were clear and the possible solutions as well, but the discussion took a different direction, one that I didn't like at all.

Instead of addressing the problem directly and discuss the causes, face to face, with the responsible, we opted for a more diplomatic way, we share the responsibility of the mistakes of few ones, among all of us.

I agreed to follow that line because I thought it could be positive for the overall mood of the team.

But suddenly, Doris, willing to start a discussion, started to question about the performance of our department and the level of our commitment.

No one doubted that our work was good so far. We had, indeed, nothing to do with the project's problems neither the delay.

But Doris opted for an easier way out, a coward on I would say. She decide to blame someone who, even if he wouldn't deserve it, would never be able to discredit her in front of the bosses.

My first reaction was surprise, I wanted to believe it was part of the process of reflection and explained what out department had done, what was good and what could be improved to be more efficient.

But my surprise turned to disappointment when Doris took our ideas on further improvements as the cause of the current problems. It wasn't fair. Neither true.

I responded as calmly as I could, but she was sure to be right so she insisted: "No, seriously, tell us why those improvements were not implemented so far, you would be more efficient and faster".

"Seriously, do you want to discuss that? now?" I asked her.

"I don't see why not, that's why we are here" she replied.

And I realized that I was about to loose control, I would explode, so all I could do was measure my words in order to minimize the damage.

"We haven't implemented those improvements because we always had higher priority tasks. You imply that the delay is our fault but you don't say anything about the real causes of the problems. We could review past meetings, it's all there".

"That would take ages..."

"But that's why we are here, right?"

After a pause I continued "But anyway, I guess it's easier to blame our department instead of explaining why you didn't notify this problem weeks ago. That would be something to discuss, but here we are, talking about issues that don't lead us anywhere. Sorry but you're not right, and I'm leaving now, I have another meeting much more important than this one".

When I got up, I could see on the faces of the people there that they were agreed. Doris, wounded, refused to accept the defeat and tried to replicate once again: "What meeting can be more important than this one?"

At that time, in the middle of a rush of and knowing that the team was on my side I said:"I'm meeting a girl that I've met. She is the best thing that happened to me lately. So yes, meeting her is more important to me that this discussion".

I got up and left. I went downstairs with so much energy and anger inside me that I thought I could do anything.

And that was when the universe acted and gave me an opportunity.

Because I deserved. Because I could seize it. Near the coffee area I saw the old man wandering aimlessly, he had seen the Austrian girl there, waiting, so he was just walking around and staring.

I took a little detour and there she was, waiting for me near to the coffee machine and the old man few meters behind her. She cheerfully greeted me but I barely looked at her, I had another target in my mind. And a lot of fury inside me.

I walked towards the man, aware that my expression and body language showed extreme aggressiveness. From his face I knew he was surprised and somewhat intimidated. I stood in front of him and said: "Hello, everything alright"?.

"Yes, yes, of course" he replied.

And the man left. I headed then towards my Austrian girl while she looked at me completely surprised.

"What is with you?" she said.

"I just have a lot of accumulated fury, I need to smash something, to destroy something grrr" I shouted.

The man wasn't yet close enough to heard me, I turned around and he was looking at me, a bit scared, so I said: "Now tell me, what problem do you with this girl"?

He didn't expect that, didn't know even what to that answer to that. He just turned around and left. The look of the girl, surprised, happy, shocked, was certainly something I will never forget.

She told me afterwards that, from that moment the old man didn't bother her anymore. Whenever they met, he simply looked down and pretended not having seen her.

10 | The austrian girl

We started to meet each time more often with the excuse of improving my German. At that point, I had already completely abandoned the tandems. They had worked very well but now, I could talk decently and the idea that motivated me the most was talking to my Austrian girl.

Barnie saw me ofter talking to her, but he never asked me about her. I think he needed time to assimilate that he was wrong when he explained to me, back when we met, that the Spaniards had no chance with the Austrian woman, specially in comparison with the Austrian guys.

Neither did I try to talk to Barnie about it, mainly because there wasn't so much to tell. We met, talked some German for me, some English for her.

After a while, he became interested in learning Spanish so I gave her some very basic classes, just to introduced her to the language.

We went one day for a walk around the town, enjoying the good weather, and we found a group of young girls on the sidewalk, selling different things. From lucky stones till garden flowers.

We approached them, the girls would be 6-7 years old, and with the best German that I could deploy, I started talking with the older one, which most likely seemed to understand me, I thought.

"Hello, I would like to buy a lucky stone, but first I want to know how much they cost" I told her.

"We have different sizes, the small ones have less luck but they're cheap, the big ones have a lot of luck so they cost more" she answered me.

I looked up and the girl looked me, up and down, until she told me: "I think that you need a lot of luck so you should buy the biggest one".

"You mean, the most expensive?"

"Well, it's up to you if you want to be lucky or not".

I found myself looking for coins in my pocket and hoping she would accept my money. I took the stone and me and my girl, continue with the walk. Afterwards, when passed again the same street, the girls were still there.

My Austrian girl didn't realize so I took my chance, when I was sure the girls had seen me, I took her energetically gave her a kiss. like in the movies.

She wasn't expected that, but as I smiled, I lifted the stone and shouted at the girls: "Thank you, it really works!".

We also did other things together, like sports. I invited her once to joins us, Rafa and me, to go climbing because I knew she liked it.

Rafa barely knew her, just talked to her few times so he had no idea that she already coudl speak a bit of Spanish.

We took the bus to go to the climbing hall, and after some minutes she looked at me and said in Spanish: "now, do it".

Rafa, puzzled, looked at her while I took my phone and started filming. The girl started talking to him in perfect Spanish, a typical kids game:

"I see something, I see something" she said to Rafa.

"What do you see?" replied him.

"One little thing".

"What little thing is that?"

"It starts with... R!".

Rafawas still wondering how she could know that kids riddle, so I replied: "Rafa!!"

"Yes! correct!" said the girl.

The expression of Rafa was a poem, he didn't even noticed that it was recording everything, he just looked dumbfounded at the girl. Until he finally woke up, he looked at me and started laughing.

By then, I had already told Corbalán about my Austrian girl and I noticed that the tone of his answers was different when we talked about her.

He seemed more paternal, more excited, I think he wanted me to realized that, at the end of the day, the most important thing was her.

In the past months, I had faced all sorts of problems and adventures. I had achieved success in many different areas but none of that could compare to find the girl I had found. And Corbalán knew that. He knew me well enough to be aware of the magnitude of that. That was why he was so happy in his emails.

Until that moment, I had never considered the possibility of meeting Corbalán in person. I had used to communicate with him by email. It was already part of our story. But now I really wanted to introduce him to my Austrian girl, so they could meet each other, and I could thank him in person for all the good advices he had given me till then.

But to my surpriseCorbalán rejected the invitation. His arguments, not very specific, implied that maybe he wasn't able to travel a lot.

I didn't want to dig deeper into the subject because I felt that if he didn't give me explanations was because didn't want to, maybe it wasn't pleasant for him to talk about it. So I answered politely, offering to help in whatever he could possibly need.

The summer I spent with my Austrian girl was amazing. He forced me to do things I had always wanted to do but had never decided to try. We got along very well and enjoyed doing all kinds of things together.

One of the things I loved to do with her was watching football games. She wasn't really passionate for football, but she used to identified with some teams for the most peculiar reasons.

One day I found her watching a game cheering like crazy a German team. I asked her: "why do you support them instead of an Austrian team", to which she answered that when she was a child she had a shirt quite similar with the same colors, therefore she must support them. Simple and powerful.

That summer, the Eurocup was taking place in France, in which Spain and Austria were participating. We decided to watch the games together whenever possible.

We couldn't make it till the last qualifiers day. Austria wasn't doing well, they needed that Portugal didn't win. We were to watch the game of Portugal and she was excited, every failure, every action was for here like a matter of life and death.

In the first half, Portugal scored and while the players were celebrating and laughing, she released all her anger: "that's it, celebrate now because in the next round you will defeated by Spain and you will cry like babies".

I didn't know whether to laugh or to ask her if she was okay. She didn't even give me the option, she came to me, defeated and said "come on, hug me, these guys don't give anything but dissatisfactions".

Summer passed by really fast, certainly one of the best that I remember in Vorarlberg. We started preparing the Christmas holidays, that year she would come with me to Spain.

She had never been there before so she was really excited about that trip. Furthermore, she was progressing with the language which motivated her even more.

The day we were flying to Spain, she was so nervous that she woke up even before the alarm went off. She had spent the last weeks immersed in Spanish books, dictionaries and grammars.

She really wanted to make a good impression in my family. It didn't matter to her that I repeated a thousand times that she shouldn't worry about anything, not even by language since she could speak quite well at that time. But she, with that passion and that ambition that once made me fall in love, wanted to talk to everyone in Spanish at the highest level possible.

On our way to the airport I sent one last email to Corbalán, congratulating the holidays and wishing him the best for the new year. I was aware that, at least for the moment, we wouldn't meet. But I got no answer. I really hoped that he was alright.

We arrived at the airport and as expected, it was really crowded. We had to wait a couple of hours until the boarding gate were opened, so we went for a drink. Sitting there while having coffee, she asked me: "what is wrong? you are very quiet".

"Yes, it's because of Corbalán. I'm worried about him".

"Well, I also wanted to know him but don't worry, I'm sure he is fine".

But I wasn't so sure, the more I thought about it, the more I feared the worst. It was then when in the distance, among the crowd, I thought I had seen a familiar face.

I thought that I was confused, it disappeared, but seconds later the cloud of people cleared for an instant and there it was again. It couldn't be true, I knew it couldn't be him.

But my eyes swore they were seeing Corbalán, there, at the airport, standing up flipping through some magazines. My brain, instead, swore that it wasn't possible.

I went over to see if it was really him, but a new wave of people made me loose the eye contact for a moment. And he wasn't there. I walked around but couldn't find him.

I went back to my girl, thinking about what just happened. I was really convinced it was him. I couldn't help walking around a bit more, draining the last chances to find him behind a corner. No sign of Corbalán anywhere.

My girl didn't even realized that I was back, she was concentrated reading through a book.

I tried to tell her that I thought I had seenCorbalán, but she ignored me, still immersed in her reading. I realized that she was happier than minutes before,"studying Spanish and so happy?, that can't be true" I thought.

I asked her and she said that she was so happy because of the book she was reading. That sounded strange to me, I checked the book but didn't recognize it. It was a book with notes, drawings and sketches made by hand. Sure it wasn't mine, but from where she had taken, was still a mystery to me.

"And this book, where did you get it?"

"Ah, while you were gone, a man approached and saw me studying Spanish. He told me all I needed to learn was in this book and he gave it to me. It contains many things that I don't understand but it's really interesting".

I picked up the book and started reading. I knew that collection of sentences, that style. I kept reading and I had no doubt, there were the same advices that Corbalán had given to me over the years. I looked at my girl and asked: "And that man, didn't say anything else"?

She thought for a moment and replied: "Yes, before he left, he said something in German that made no sense to me. He just said that I would understand it in future".

"What was that then?"

He said, "Das Leben ist gut, you'll decide how your life is going to be, only you. Never forget that".

Printed in Great Britain
by Amazon